Toronto. You know its skyline: the CN Tower, the high-rises, the sharp geometry of glass and steel. But the city reveals its true character at street level where its many worlds begin to overlap. And it's everywhere.

Caribbean bakeries share blocks with Michelin-starred dining rooms. Victorian storefronts hide world-class cocktail bars. Streetcars rattle past late-night noodle shops. Patios spill out onto the sidewalks. Murals stretch across laneways. Food markets buzz with a dozen languages.

LOST iN explores a Toronto where boundaries blur and boxes are made to be broken. You'll discover a speakeasy in an art gallery, Asian flavors in Italian classics, vinyl DJs in a wine bar, rare books in a vending machine, and a night market in a neon-lit basement. Along the way, you'll meet quiet radicals and loud subcultures, landmark design and unexpected wilderness, and a back alley that reminds everyone who won the Graffiti War.

Forget what you think you know about the North. Get lost in the Toronto that packs the world into a single street.

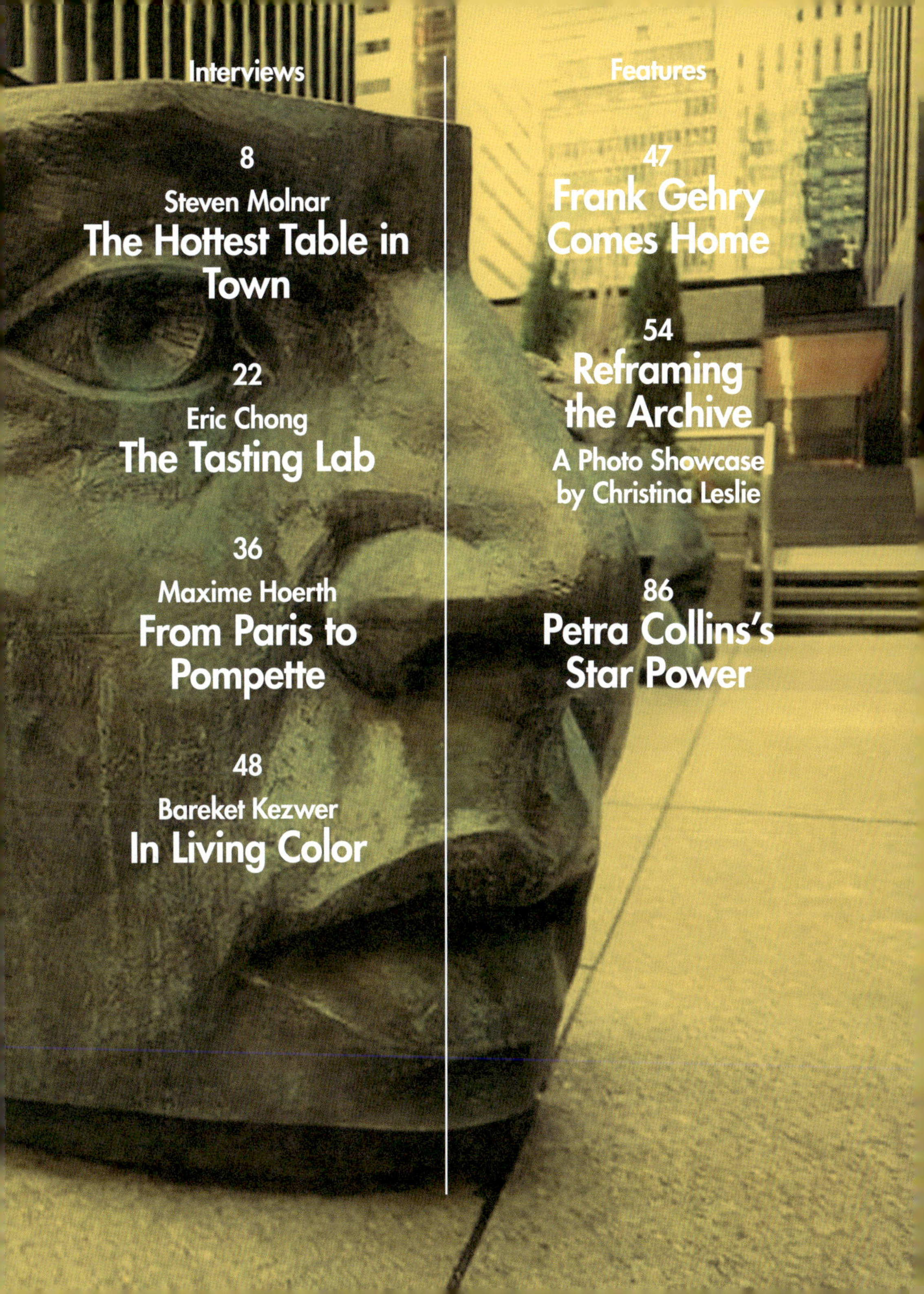

Interviews

Features

Past Meets Future

The *Royal Ontario Museum* spans natural history and world cultures, with highlights ranging from dinosaur skeletons to Egyptian mummies. The building itself is a fusion of two eras: the 1914 structure, with its mosaic-domed rotunda, and Daniel Libeskind's 2007 addition, the Michael Lee-Chin Crystal. Composed of five jagged volumes of glass and aluminum, the Crystal appears to crash straight through the older stone facade, a form inspired by crystals in the museum's own mineral collection. Inside, bridges and walkways cut at odd angles, with glimpses down into the collections below.

• Royal Ontario Museum, 100 Queen's Park, Bloor-Yorkville, rom.on.ca

Photo: Roman Slavik

Top Five

Bucket. Meet list.

Divey Bars

- ☐ Sneaky Dee's
- ☐ Farside
- ☐ Wide Open
- ☐ Lloyd's
- ☐ Swan Dive

Vinyl Shops

- ☐ She Said Boom
- ☐ Invisible City
- ☐ Sonic Boom
- ☐ Baxters Vinyl
- ☐ Neurotica Records

Freshly Shucked

- ☐ Oyster Boy
- ☐ Pearl Diver
- ☐ Island Oysters at Waterworks
- ☐ Pure Spirits
- ☐ Anglr

Sidewalk Shoots

- ☐ Gooderham Building
- ☐ Toronto Music Garden
- ☐ Allan Gardens
- ☐ Bathurst Street Bridge
- ☐ Kensington Market

Street Canvases

- ☐ Rush Lane (Graffiti Alley)
- ☐ Underpass Park
- ☐ Kensington Market Alleys
- ☐ The Reggae Lane Mural
- ☐ The Keele Wall (RIP)

Maple Leafs Hockey Brawls

- [ ] Buffalo Sabres (Sept. 22, 2013)
- [ ] Montreal Canadiens (Oct. 30, 1963)
- [ ] Philadelphia Flyers (March 17, 1974)
- [ ] Montreal Canadiens (April 21, 1979)
- [ ] Ottawa Senators (April 13, 2002)

Urban Escapes

- [ ] Don Valley Brick Works Park
- [ ] Rouge National Urban Park
- [ ] Crothers Woods
- [ ] Glen Stewart Ravine
- [ ] Tommy Thompson Park

Toronto Film Cameos

- [ ] *Mean Girls* (2004)
- [ ] *The Shape of Water* (2017)
- [ ] *Scott Pilgrim vs. the World* (2010)
- [ ] *Chicago* (2002)
- [ ] *The Fly* (1986)

Historic Drinking Dens

- [ ] Monarch Tavern
- [ ] Horseshoe Tavern
- [ ] The Rex Hotel Jazz & Blues Bar
- [ ] The Wheatsheaf Tavern
- [ ] Library Bar

Artist Residencies

- [ ] Gibraltar Point Centre for the Arts
- [ ] Open Studio
- [ ] Gladstone House Artist Residency
- [ ] Cedar Ridge Creative Centre
- [ ] The Bentway Artist Residency

Photo: Richard Taveira

Steven Molnar

The Hottest Table in Town

At *Quetzal*, everything begins with fire. Chef Steven Molnar cooks exclusively over a massive 28-foot open hearth, using nothing but wood fire, embers and patience to shape every plate. His Michelin-starred restaurant draws on regional Mexican traditions, from heirloom corn to house-ground moles, elevated with technique honed in top-tier French and Spanish kitchens. The result is a flame-driven experience that beautifully rewrites the rules of haute Mexican cuisine.

How does the wood fire influence the flavor and texture of your ingredients?

We only have wood fire here, no gas whatsoever. That's a level of flavor you can't really replicate any other way. We cook all of our meats indirectly with a tiered system grill. We start at the highest tier with just the wood-fire smoke and no direct contact with the flames. The smoke tenderizes the meat, allowing it to absorb a lot of flavor, and then we rest it a bit before searing it directly in the coals at the very, very bottom. This approach produces beautiful vegetables as well. We cook directly in the coals, super fast, super hard, using paddle fans to put more oxygen into the fire. It produces a beautiful smoky flavor and charred texture. If we were just sautéing on a gas grill, it wouldn't have the same effect.

What is a dish that benefits from a slow-and-low approach on the fire?

The fish. If you blast it right away, you burst the skin. I always tell the staff, "You can cook a fish in 2 minutes, but you can also cook a fish in 20 minutes." It's just how you maneuver things and work it around the fire. The goal is for the skin to be perfectly crisp, nice little bubbles, while keeping the flesh extremely juicy.

What regions of Mexico influence you the most?

Oaxaca and the Yucatán. I look forward to taking a bigger trip to Baja California to explore the seafood and wine culture. It's difficult to get certain types of alcohol in Ontario because everything is controlled by our government, but I'd like to build out a wine program here that showcases high-quality Mexican wines. I'm also starting a gin company with my bar manager and a couple of guys in Mexico City. It's made 100 percent with Oaxaca botanicals, all organic, all heirloom.

Tlayudas are my favorite dish from Oaxaca. What's the trick to making them great?

It starts with the corn, obviously. We import heirloom varieties from Mexico. Right now, we use Tuxpeño amarillo corn from Chiapas that we nixtamalize every night. We have a traditional volcanic stone *molino* from Mexico in the back of the restaurant, and we grind our masa fresh every morning. Then we use a comal, the traditional cooking surface, to create the base of the tlayuda. We get that authentic flavor because we make them exactly the same way they do in Mexico.

Oaxaca is known for its moles, and you trained in French cuisine, which is known for its sauces. How do you combine the two?

To be honest, one of the strongest points in this restaurant is the sauce game. I'm so passionate about sauces, and I think it's what really ties every dish together in the end.

When we were developing the first menu here, we opened up *Oaxaca al Gusto* by Diana Kennedy, and the very first thing I made was a traditional mole negro. Just looking at that recipe and ingredients, I realized it was going to take me about four hours. But once I gathered all the ingredients and started to put it together, I started to understand why it has so much complexity and depth of flavor. Every ingredient plays a role and has a purpose.

What are some other sauces on the menu?

For our mushroom dish, we make a crema poblana inspired by *rajas* poblanos, a chunky taco filling made of poblano strips, onions, corn and crema. We cook the base the same way, but instead of leaving it chunky, we blend it into a smooth sauce. It pairs perfectly with the mushrooms and shishito peppers.

From French cuisine, you transitioned to Spanish cuisine. How was that transition?

I worked with more sauces like *ajoblanco* and *romesco*, and we did a ton of charcuterie and curing. We were making our own chorizo, *chistorra* served with *guindilla* peppers, and even *mojama*, which is cured, air-dried tuna. I love the patience it requires, where you wait six months to try the first

slice of something you built from scratch. We also did a lot of *conservas*, packing ingredients into highly infused oils.

How does this translate to Quetzal?

When wild mushrooms are in season, I use that exact *conservas* technique, preserving them in a Mexican chili-infused oil to use three months later. We've also played with sausages here, like a Toluca-style chorizo verde. The connection between the cultures is also fascinating, learning *boudin noir* in French kitchens, *morcilla* in Spanish ones, and then seeing how Mexico does *moronga*. It's amazing how the same foundational idea transforms just by shifting the native spices, yet you yield such a different product at the end.

For someone who wants to move beyond espadin, what type of mezcal do you recommend?

Pechuga is a deeply ceremonial style of mezcal, and every batch varies wildly depending on the *mezcalero*. They use different seasonal fruits, wild herbs and an actual animal breast, whether it's turkey, chicken or rabbit, suspended inside the still. On my last trip to Oaxaca, I visited an ancestral producer named Don Pablo. He's this tiny man doing everything by hand with zero machinery, mashing agave for hours. He happened to have a batch of *pechuga* in the still right then. He pulled out the rabbit breast, and we tasted it. It was incredible. The meat had absorbed all the smoke from the wood fire and the sweetness of the dried fruits in the pot. When you explain to a guest that alcohol vapors are passing through a hanging piece of meat to capture those complex flavors, it blows their mind.

What do outsiders tend to misunderstand about the culinary cultures in Toronto?

When you travel to other global cities, you see different ethnic cuisines, but it's not at the level or quantity that we have in Toronto. We have multiple Chinatowns, Japanese and Korean areas, all these different parts of the city that showcase their cuisine and the

Seahorse
Summerhill

Bar Raval
Little Italy

Bar Pompette
Little Italy

Civil Liberties
Bloorcourt

Civil Works
Fashion District

Graffiti Alley
Fashion District

community built around that. The city's identity is woven through these neighborhoods. I'm a perfect example as someone who's half Japanese and half Hungarian, and that kind of cultural mixing is common here. That diversity fosters a unique lane of culinary creativity. Whether it's Ethiopian, Indian, Cambodian or Thai, almost every culture is represented in Toronto at a remarkably high level. That standard of authenticity and accessibility is something few other cities in the world can replicate.

Have any chefs you mentored opened their own restaurants in Toronto?

Yes. My sous chef [Federico Garcia] left last year and opened a seafood-forward restaurant called *Seahorse*. They're doing incredibly well and just won *Toronto Life*'s Best New Restaurant. He was an integral part of our team for many years, so seeing him find his own success is very rewarding. When you spend 60-plus hours a week together in a kitchen, you're constantly pushing each other to grow, learn and improve. To see his success is really amazing.

Any cocktail bars you recommend that also blend cultures?

Bar Raval is a Spanish-inspired tapas bar that does great work with its cocktail program. *Bar Pompette* is amazing and eclectic with a team from all over the world. It's owned by a French team, but the staff has bartenders from places like Ireland and Colombia.

A big one for Toronto is *Civil Liberties*, and a couple of years ago, they opened a second bar called *Civil Works*. They do something that sounds like a gimmick at first, but it's actually interesting. They take Toronto tap water and alter the pH and mineral levels to replicate water from different regions around the world. So if you're ordering a whiskey, they can serve it with exact replicas of Japanese water, Irish water, Scottish water or whatever. It gives you the closest possible experience to drinking that spirit in its home country.

Away from the kitchen, what local outdoor activities do you like?

If you go north from Toronto, there are amazing trails, caves, waterfalls, beautiful lakes and a lot of camping. My family has a cottage up in Algonquin Park, which is the biggest provincial park in Ontario. I try to get up there as much as I can to go fishing and things like that. Along the corridor of the park, there are about 30 beautiful trails that lead you through the area. The best time to go is in the fall when all the trees are changing colors. It's a great way to reconnect and slow things down a little bit.

When it comes to appreciating art, are you more of a gallery or graffiti person?

As I get older, I'm more into the gallery world, but when I was younger, I was really into street art. We have a place called *Graffiti Alley*, and a lot of tourists go there to take pictures. It's funny because right before we started this conversation, I was talking to the woman who owns this building. She was asking about graffiti artists because she wants to get a mural painted somewhere. We have some really beautiful street art that is unique to Toronto.

The World Kitchen

Toronto's food scene mirrors the city itself: layered, restless and shaped by generations of migration. Rather than chase a singular idea of Canadian cuisine, its most exciting restaurants draw on diverse cultures, memories and influences to tell personal stories through food.

Photo: Destination Toronto/Daniel Neuhaus

A Pretty Penny

Sliders, cheap drinks and a great atmosphere, the expectations are high when you enter *Pennies*, one of the city's most beloved low-cost establishments. The stars of the menu are the deliciously affordable two-bite sandwiches. Add in complimentary popcorn and nostalgic cocktails, and it's hard to find a better deal in Toronto. That is, until the almost-daily happy hour starts. Both West End locations feature the brand's signature yellow exterior and massive patios, so stop pinching your pennies, slide up to the bar and enjoy a meal that won't break the bank.

• Pennies Bellwoods, various locations, pennies.bar

Birds of a Feather

Sitting side by side, *The Wren* and *The Wood Owl* are sister restaurants with creative daily specials and unpretentious service. Always buzzing, The Wren takes no reservations and is more laid-back with a focus on Ontario craft beer and elevated pub fare like croquettes, burgers and fried chicken. You will need a reservation, however, for *The Wood Owl* (photo), which pairs a careful selection of wines with seasonal, vegetable-laden dishes like smoked trout dip. In addition to set menus, both spots announce the day's featured plate on no-nonsense Instagram profiles, often prompting a rain of salivating emojis.

• The Wood Owl/The Wren, 1380-82 Danforth Avenue, East Danforth @thewoodowlto, @thewrendanforth

Hi-Fi

Toronto's first audiophile saloon opened in 2019, completing its dishes and drinks with vinyl bliss. Inspired by traditional Japanese *kissas*, *The Little Jerry* is a bar designed to create an audiophile's dream aural experience. No stale playlists or algorithms here. Every vinyl record is handpicked by the staff, and guest DJs spin tracks to elevate the atmosphere while you sip. But the drinks don't play second fiddle. The meticulously curated menu features fine wines, crisp beers and a selection of vermouths for an evening smoother than Smokey Robinson.

• The Little Jerry, 418 College Street, University, thelittlejerry.com

Photo: The Little Jerry

Love Letter to Portugal

There's no online menu for this intentionally elusive space, as if to say, "Trust us, just book it," and you should. The chilled octopus is as refreshing as a sea dip, and you'll want to sop up every last drop of the paprika-spiked sauces. Co-owner Kelly Amaral, inspired by memories of her Azorean parents' Portuguese grocery store nearby, has created a space to linger as if on Portuguese time. Whether you come for a dimly lit date or an evening on the spacious rooftop, you'll find yourself ordering endless croquetas and aguardiente cocktails.

• Taberna LX, 1161 Dundas Street West, Little Portugal, tabernalx.com

Souls Intertwined

Like his Jamaican-Chinese heritage, *MasterChef Canada* judge Craig Wong proves that Caribbean and Asian flavors were meant for each other at *Patois*, his original Toronto restaurant. More than a decade later, it remains the go-to spot for the juiciest jerk chicken, served straight up or tangled through chow mein. Then there's the izakaya shrimp pasta, tossed in the restaurant's closely guarded spice blend, and its signature fried chicken with an impossibly thin, shatter-crisp crust. If you want the full experience, order the family-style Whole Shebang feast and wash it down with a Pink Ting.

• Patois, 794 Dundas Street West, Trinity Bellwoods, patoistoronto.com

Photos: Adam Freire, Denis Gutierrez-Ogrinc

Jerk & Juice

Some restaurants transport you. *Chubby's* practically hands you a plane ticket. From the reggae soundtrack to the scent of jerk smoke, this laid-back Caribbean spot feels like a mini escape. The menu puts playful spins on Jamaican classics, from saltfish fritters with mango-lime-papaya salsa to slow-baked jerk wings dosed with scotch bonnet. There's even oxtail poutine. Settle in during happy hour with a woozy pitcher of rum punch or a bucket of Red Stripe. You know the vibe is right when the house Spotify playlist has more than 400 saves.

• Chubby's Jamaican Kitchen, 104 Portland Street, Yorkville, chubbysjamaican.com

The Royal Treatment

Open shutters by day, soft lighting by night and green velvet banquettes beckon at any hour. Surrendering your palate at *Kiin* comes easily, thanks to married owners chef Nuit Regular and restaurateur Jeff Regular (PAI, Sukhothai), whose Michelin-recognized approach brings royal Thai cuisine to the forefront. The kitchen's seasonal menu showcases refined dishes once served in Thailand's royal courts, balancing intricate flavors with broad appeal. Order à la carte or settle in for the seven-course tasting menu. Either way, you'll venture beyond the usual suspects while comfortably holding crowd-pleaser status.

• Kiin, 323 Adelaide Street West, Entertainment District, kiintoronto.com

Photos: Ryan Lee/Destination Toronto

Poetic Plates

A giant glass mosaic of Kate Bush and Virginia Woolf dressed in angelic regalia presides over this candlelit Leslieville favorite. Handwritten menus detail a rotating slate of inventive small plates, with past offerings that range from sausage-stuffed morels and pumpkin nachos to poached-lobster ramen. Poetry informs the tasting notes on the wine list, reinforcing the nostalgic literary vibe. From May to November on the patio, the reservation-only mystery tasting menu is legendary, with stories woven into every course. For cocktails, head next door to the restaurant's self-described weird sibling, *Belle Isle*.

• Lake Inez, 1471 Gerrard Street East, Leslieville, lakeinezto.com

Photo: Scarlet O'Neill

Taste the Tide

Rodney's Oyster House has been a Toronto staple since 1987. Founded by the late, great Rodney Clark, the sprawling basement restaurant is filled with the city's finest seafood. Despite the quality of the menu, the space is unpretentious and friendly, with warm wooden walls teeming with oyster shells signed by celebrity fans. The seasonal menu varies with coastal fishing quotas, but between 9 and 26 oyster varieties are available daily. Snag a spot at the bar for a front-row seat to raw delight.

• Rodney's Oyster House, 469 King Street West, Wellington Place, rodneysoysterhouse.com

Italy Heads East

First- and second-generation chefs in Toronto grew up straddling multiple food cultures. They may have trained in French or Italian kitchens, but their palates were built on Jamaican oxtail, Filipino adobo and Jewish brisket. Toronto's postwar Italian diaspora, one of the largest migration waves in Canadian history, brought starch- and dough-based traditions that offer chefs a versatile canvas for reinvention. These kitchens lead the way, with several clustered together on the same strip in Little Italy.

Photo: Nicole & Baaal

Hong Kong to Queen West

Liliana pairs the structure of a classic trattoria with subtle Asian influences shaped by chef Marvin Palomo's Filipino heritage and his formative years in Hong Kong, where he worked at the Michelin-starred *Vea*, known for its refined fusion of French and Chinese traditions. The Liliana menu stays rooted in Italian technique with pastas, crudo and seasonal proteins, but the flavors are quietly reframed with ingredients like miso, furikake and yuzu koshō. Dishes can range from stuffed chicken wings with carnaroli rice and black truffle to tiger shrimp with Manila clams and Tokyo turnip.

• Liliana, 1198 Queen Street West, West Queen West, lilianatoronto.com

Itameshi in Little Italy

Housed inside a restored heritage bank building, *DaNico* elegantly captures the *itameshi* trend, a form of Japanese-Italian fusion started in Tokyo in the 1990s. Naples-born Daniele Corona previously worked at top fine-dining restaurants in Milan and Rome before coming to Toronto and becoming the first Italian chef in Canada with Michelin stars at multiple restaurants. This includes DaNico, which serves seasonal courses like fettuccine topped with Japanese tuna tartare and charcoal-grilled wagyu with shisito pepper and fresh wasabi.

• DaNico, 440 College Street, Little Italy, danicotoronto.com

Pasta & Dashi

Radici Project focuses its menu around seasonal Canadian ingredients, also expressed through an *itameshi* lens that blends technique and flavor traditions from both cultures. Dishes move between delicate dashi, house-made pastas and sake pairings, reflecting a shared culinary language rather than a forced fusion. The result is a tightly edited tasting experience shaped by two culinary worlds in constant conversation.

• Radici Project, 588 College Street, Little Italy, radiciproject.ca

Photo: Daniel Neuhaus

Diaspora Crossings

Powered by a charcoal grill and a taste for nostalgic flavors, *N.L. Ginzburg* filters traditional trattoria fare through Italian and Jewish diasporic traditions. Handmade pastas, chicken liver crostini and seasonal Ontario ingredients reveal subtle connections between the cuisines, while the restaurant's name honors Italian-Jewish anti-fascists Natalia and Leone Ginzburg. Rather than chasing strict authenticity, N.L. Ginzburg embraces a distinctly Toronto sensibility: rooted in heritage, shaped by migration and open to reinvention.

• N.L. Ginzburg, 548 College Street, Little Italy, nlginzburg.com

Eric Chong

The Tasting Lab

Eric Chong is no stranger to pressure. After winning the inaugural season of *MasterChef Canada*, the former chemical engineer went on to establish himself as one of the most inventive chefs in the city. Collaborating with his fiery mentor, Alvin Leung, he opened the Asian-fusion *R&D* with signature dishes like roasted Peking duck and his competition-winning lobster chow mein. He followed with *aKin*, a Michelin-starred restaurant with tasting menus rooted in playful nostalgia and storytelling.

You're known for creative menus at aKin with fun themes like Chinese takeout food.

We try to create modern takes on classic nostalgia dishes that non-Asians would know. I think it creates a more memorable dining experience when a guest can relate to the original dish, and it showcases our creativity. We want guests to say, "I've had this before, but I've never had it in this form."

What inspired this?

I've been fortunate enough to dine in many Michelin restaurants, and one of them was a Latin American restaurant called *MONO* in Hong Kong. It was incredible, but everything was so foreign that they actually gave the guests an encyclopedia with all the terms and ingredients. My chef-mentor, Alvin, asked me the next day, "What did you have?" I had to say, "I don't know." That was the last thing I wanted for aKin.

The previous menu was inspired by the Chinese New Year, which was very Chinese culture–focused. I felt like it segregated a lot of non-Asians. I wanted the next menu to be as welcoming as possible. I think Western Chinese is something everybody knows. Everybody knows Kung Pao chicken, chow mein, Yangchow fried rice, hot and sour soup, sweet and sour pork, so it's very relatable, and it was very well received.

What have been some of the more popular menu themes?

Our dim sum–inspired menu, as well as a street food menu where we featured a lot of Southeast Asian dishes. We did a fun aphrodisiac-inspired menu around Valentine's. Long tasting menus tend to stay

Photos: Nicole & Bcgol

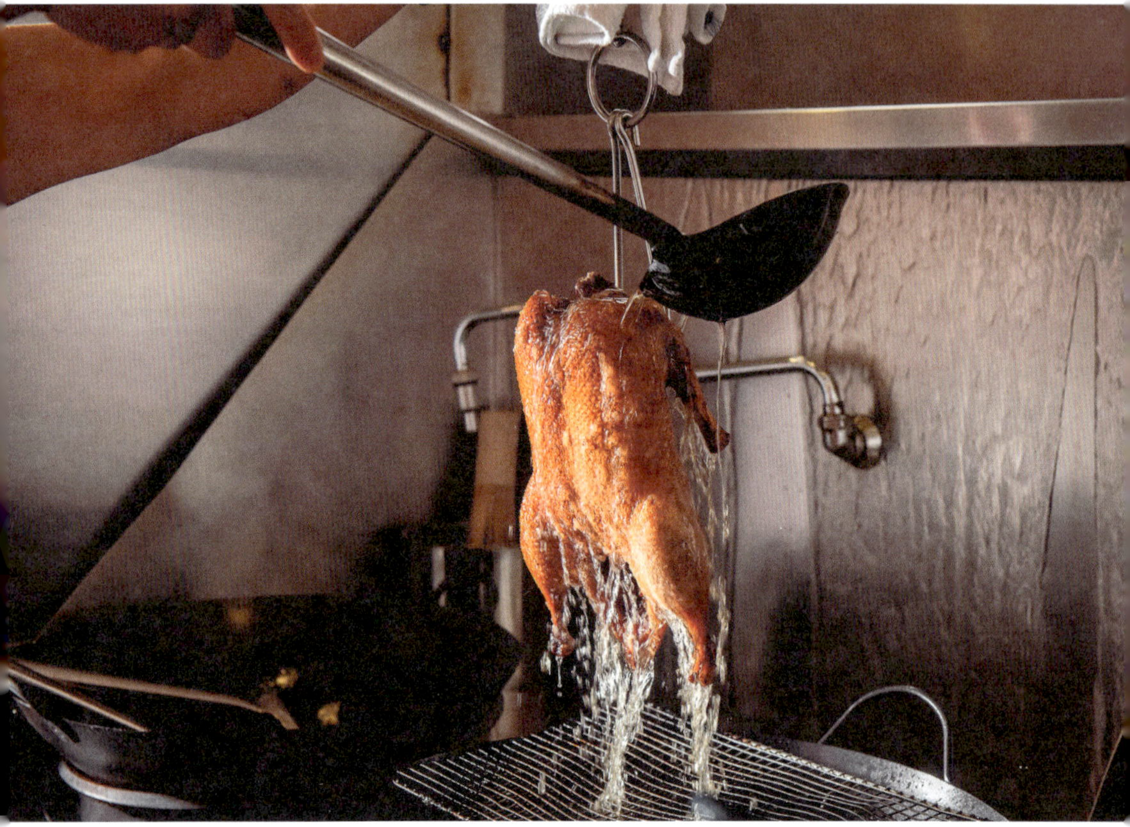

stagnant, with maybe one or two dishes getting swapped out, but we change all ten courses each time. We're currently on our ninth menu in 18 months.

What dishes were on the aphrodisiac menu?

Oysters, for one. One of the petit fours was a cherry tart with pop rocks on it. I thought popping the cherry was funny, but not a lot of people got it.

Most fine-dining restaurants have wine pairings, but aKin also has cocktails. How do you pair cocktails with food?

When we start developing a new menu, we explain the theme to the bar team and let them taste our sauces. Every single cocktail is specifically made just for the dish. Every menu has a "sphere" course, and right now it's our hot and sour soup. It's served in a yin-yang pattern—one half hot and the other half sour. The soup is usually quite umami and spicy, so you want something more refreshing and cooling to balance it. We paired it with a passion fruit daiquiri made with clarified passion fruit syrup, white rum and chamomile tea.

The chow mein is also quite spicy, so we pair it with a soothing margarita. Our salt-and-pepper squid dish is paired with a cocktail that has Szechuan peppercorn oil in it. Sometimes you want to echo the flavors, and sometimes you want to complement them.

Your mentor, Alvin Leung, is known as the "Demon Chef." Is that a joke or a warning?

He just takes his work very seriously, but it's not the type of person he is outside of the kitchen. I mean, you don't get three Michelin stars without the constant pursuit of perfection, and perfection demands being strict. Outside of the kitchen, he is one of the most generous, funniest people I've ever met.

You famously won the inaugural season of MasterChef Canada *at age 21. How is the pressure different when cooking on television?*

It was definitely one of the most pressure-driven environments I've ever experienced in my life. My whole future, my hopes and dreams, were tied up in this one show. If I didn't win, there was no way my parents were going to support me being a chef instead of a chemical engineer. One mistake could change the path of my life forever. I don't think anybody understands this level of pressure, where these six weeks can change your whole life.

Photos: Nicole & Bagel

Fat Rabbit
St. Catharines

CN Tower
Entertainment District

Suite 115
Little Italy

Rebel
Port Lands

How would you describe the Toronto food scene at this moment and how it differentiates itself from other big cities?

Everybody always says multicultural, but I genuinely think everybody likes to immigrate to Canada because it's so peaceful. You have incredible omakase, French food, Italian food, Indian food, fine dining, a little bit of all cultures. The advantage of Toronto is that you can get tasting menus at an incredible price.

If I want to experience emerging talent in Toronto, am I looking at street food? Bistros?

You'll find emerging talent by looking at the tasting menus, to be honest. That's the best way for chefs to express their creativity, their passion, their talent. It's hard to showcase that in like a high-paced à la carte format when you're just turning and burning tables. One exception is Zach Smith, a talented chef who doesn't do a tasting menu. He manages a few projects, but he's really known for *Fat Rabbit*. It's on the outskirts of Toronto, down in the St. Catharines area, and he does amazing things with casual, whole-animal butchery. It's just simple food, but nobody does it quite like him. He does this incredible foie gras sticky toffee pudding that is just unreal.

Where do you go on a day off?

I spend as much time with my family as possible, but when we do go out, I make an effort to try a new restaurant. Alvin always taught me, you should always be tasting what's out there, tasting the competition, tasting the trends. I feel like not enough chefs actually make that effort.

Any recommendations outside of restaurants?

I wouldn't advocate going to the *CN Tower* unless you want to get rinsed. You have to pay like 50 bucks just to go up.

Do you have a favorite bar?

Suite 115 is incredible. It's a bespoke bar where you have to enter a code to get in. If you're into nightlife and clubbing, *Rebel* is one of the best nightclubs I've ever been to in the world.

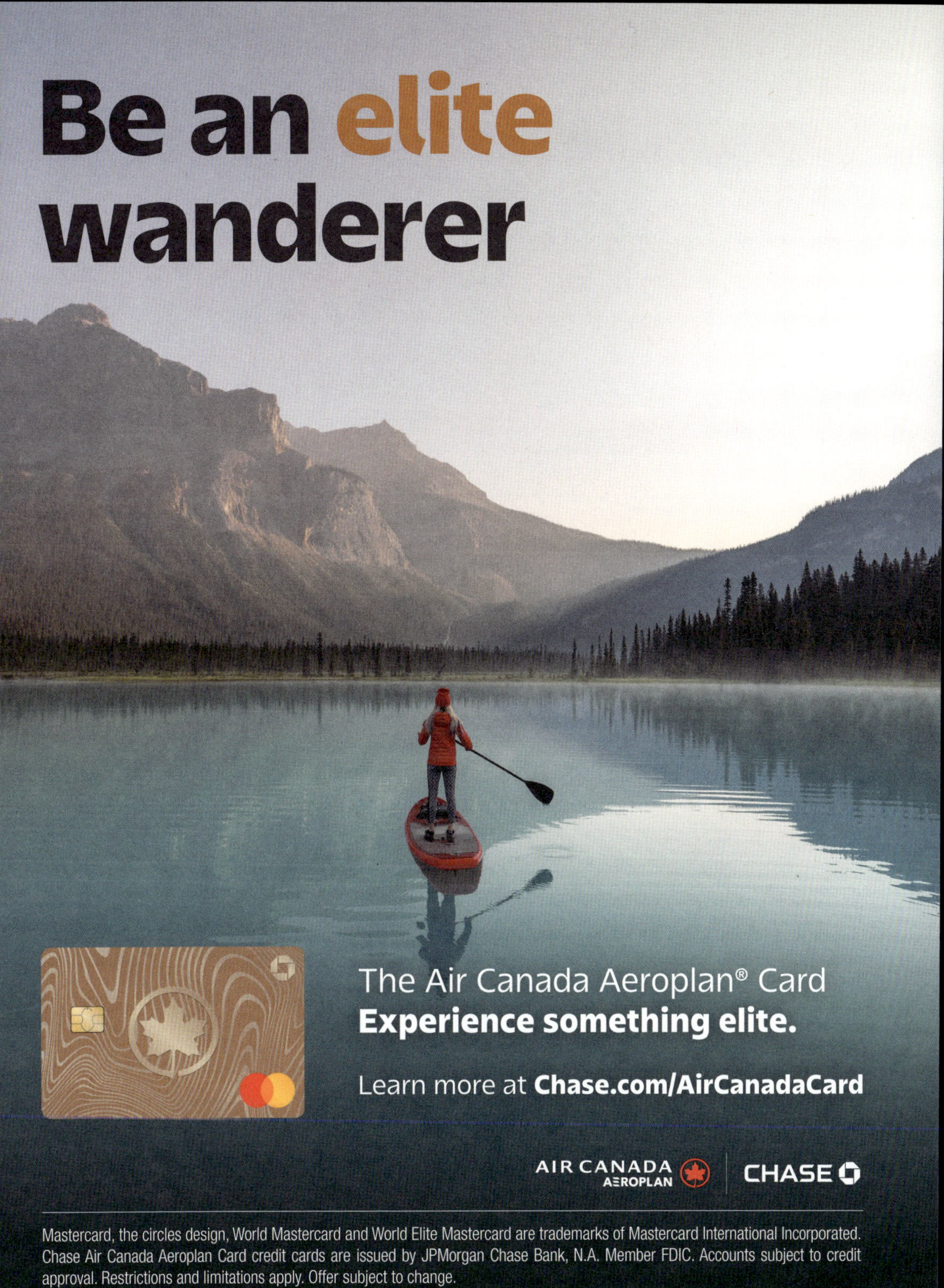
Be an elite wanderer
The Air Canada Aeroplan® Card
Experience something elite.
Learn more at Chase.com/AirCanadaCard
AIR CANADA AEROPLAN
CHASE
Mastercard, the circles design, World Mastercard and World Elite Mastercard are trademarks of Mastercard International Incorporated. Chase Air Canada Aeroplan Card credit cards are issued by JPMorgan Chase Bank, N.A. Member FDIC. Accounts subject to credit approval. Restrictions and limitations apply. Offer subject to change.

Karaoke Party

With a visual aesthetic inspired by filmmaker Wes Anderson, *Bar Mordecai* is one of Toronto's top spots for eclectic tapas and delicious cocktails. But head down the stairs and past the Green Room bar, and you'll find yourself transported to a karaoke wonderland. Four vibrant private karaoke rooms, each inspired by a musical era, offer groups the perfect environment to put on a post-dinner show. Leopard-print walls, neon signs and gold statues will put anyone in a party mood, so book your space and prepare to belt your heart out.

• Bar Mordecai, 1272 Dundas Street West, Little Portugal, barmordecai.com

Sips

The Night Shift

The bar scene thrives on contrast, where design-forward lounges share the pavement with low-key neighborhood hideaways. Across the city, the glass in front of you is just one piece of a larger narrative shaped by craft cocktails, slick speakeasies and late-night energy.

Night Market Nightcaps

Built around the concept of a bustling late-night Asian market reimagined as a neon-drenched cocktail lounge, *Midnight Market* offers an immersive escape in the heart of Little Italy. Wander through a series of interconnected spaces, from intimate cocktail corners to high-energy music dens, to find the space that fits your mood. Then settle in for Asian-forward drinks, shareable snack plates and a playful interior design. Open late, it has become a go-to spot for groups wanting something more transportive than a typical bar experience.

• Midnight Market, 434 College Street, Little Italy, midnightmkt.ca

Photo: Daniel Neuhaus/Destination Toronto

Mother Knows Best

Few Toronto bars have helped redefine cocktail culture quite like *Mother*. The Queen Street West bar has earned international acclaim for its inventive drinks and uncompromising commitment to sustainability. Ingredients that might otherwise be discarded are transformed into syrups, ferments and unexpected flavor combinations, resulting in cocktails that are virtuous, yes, but feel genuinely original as well. The room itself is intimate and dimly lit, letting the drinks take center stage. Come curious and expect the unexpected. *Mother* is the kind of place that changes how you think about cocktails.

• Mother, 874 Queen Street West, Trinity-Bellwoods, motherdrinks.co

Conversation Starters

No menu, no signatures, no fuss. At *Civil Liberties*, the bartenders start with a conversation about what flavors you enjoy and what mood you're in before building a cocktail tailored to the moment. Opened in 2014, the bar has become one of Toronto's most influential drinking destinations, helping define a more relaxed, hospitality-led approach to cocktails. The room itself is understated and welcoming, with a long bar, exposed brick and a crowd that ranges from industry regulars to first-time visitors. Trust the bartenders and let the evening unfold from there.

• Civil Liberties, 878 Bloor Street West, Bloorcourt, @civlibto

An Ethereal Escape

Tucked into an unassuming grocery storefront on the corner of a quiet block, *bosque* seems to float in another world. Its dramatic lighting imbues the bar's rich woodwork with a twilight glow. The cocktail selection is elegantly tight, showcasing creations like Doves in the Wind, a blend of fig leaf tequila, fig leaf cordial and dry curaçao; Back to Baies-sics, a blackberry gin soda freshened up with a basil tincture; and Suede on the Inside, a nitro espresso martini made with Vietnamese-style coffee. The bar also sports a curated rotation of local taps and Belgian Trappist ales.

• bosque, 940 Broadview Avenue, Playter Estates, @bosquebroadview

Photo: Brandon Barre

Getting Lit

Step into Toronto's famous *Library Bar*, and you'll feel like you've waltzed into the pages of your favorite novel. Widely considered one of Canada's best, the cocktail lounge is designed to resemble a stately library—all tufted leather benches, velvet chairs and moody lighting. Inside these storied walls, you'll find the birthplace of the iconic Bird Bath martini, alongside dozens of the best whiskeys on the market. The cocktail menu is inspired by Canadian–Sri Lankan author Michael Ondaatje's novel *In the Skin of a Lion*, promising a story with every sip.

• Library Bar, 100 Front Street West, Yonge-Bay Corridor, librarybartoronto.com

Ambience Done Right

Done Right Inn has been serving locals since 1998. Its extra-long bar boasts plenty of seats, while the leafy, secluded back patio is one of Toronto's very best. TVs sporadically show sports (including their beloved Tottenham Hotspur F.C.), but you're more likely to be taken in by the kitschy art and unpretentious atmosphere than anything else. The bartenders are amazing and know how to handle a crowd, but mind your p's and q's. No one's above the vibe.

• Done Right Inn, 861 Queen Street West, West Queen West, @thedonerightinn

Get Fixed

In the heart of Little Italy, *Ted's* is a bad-ass rock 'n' roll haven, dimly lit and gnarled to the core. The space is long and expansive, with two pool tables, a pinball machine and two patios. The soundtrack is always killer, the dripping candles are primo ambiance and the Big Bottles (you'll know 'em when you see 'em) are the perfect accoutrement to any hang. It's cash-only, but there's an ATM on-site. Whether you're a hipster, lover or punk, come prepared to stay awhile.

• Ted's Collision, 573 College Street, Little Italy

Enter Differently

Sometimes the best nights have no front door.

Behind the Curtain

Hidden inside the *Coffee Oysters Champagne* bar, *à toi* is Toronto's most theatrical speakeasy: a 1920s-inspired cocktail den staffed by characters in period costume, with hush-hush side rooms that might reveal tarot readings, burlesque or an immersive theatrical production modeled on New York's *Sleep No More*. Ask for a "champagne tour" to find the discreet and anything but quiet spot: low lighting, rich jewel tones and a soundtrack that pulls you deeper into the fantasy with every round. This is one of the city's most fully realized nights out, gimmicks very much included.

• à toi, 214 King Street West, Entertainment District, sipshucksip.com/a-toi

A Sultry Secret

Some of the best nights begin with an unmarked staircase, and you'll find this particular set of stairs in a Michelin-listed restaurant. Unlike the crisp lines and white tablecloths of *GEORGE Restaurant*, the scene upstairs in *Secrette* is all texture and warmth. Rich velvets and vibrant colors playfully interact with a whimsical wallpaper of framed bunny photos designed by Neo-Expressionist artist Hunt Slonem. The eccentric and lush vibe is paired with a seasonal small-bites menu and meticulously made cocktails, creating an approachable and exciting space to while away the hours with friends.

• Secrette, 111C Queen Street East, Moss Park, secretteonqueen.com

A Cut Above

Amid the hustle and bustle of Ossington Avenue lies one of Toronto's worst-kept secrets. At a glance, it's a classic barbershop, woefully abandoned past 7:30pm. But go beyond those swiveling chairs and through a beaded curtain to be transported to the retro speakeasy of your dreams. *Gift Shop* is a small venue with a massive menu, showcasing carefully curated spirits and mouthwateringly creative libations. Arrive early or be ready to wait. With only 16 seats and a stellar reputation, this gift shop isn't one to skip.

• Gift Shop, 89 Ossington Avenue, Trinity Bellwoods, freehouse.co/locations/gift-shop

Art of the Cocktail

Toronto's West End is an ever-expanding hub of arts and food culture, but it long lacked a space where the two truly intersect. Enter *Cry Baby Gallery*, an intimate cocktail bar concealed within a contemporary art space. Every step from the narrow, whitewashed gallery to the seductively curved, backlit bar feels like the epitome of cool-kid culture. The menus read like an art-stylized Yellow Pages, featuring complex drinks with handcrafted elements laid out alongside bold graphics and eye-catching designs. Peruse the art, have a sip and embrace your inner "it girl."

• Cry Baby Gallery, 1468 Dundas Street West, Little Portugal, crybabygallery.ca

Photo Rick O'Brien

Maxime Hoerth

From Paris to Pompette

Bar Pompette **has set a new standard for craft cocktails in Toronto, led by acclaimed mixologist Maxime Hoerth. After helming some of the top bars in Paris and becoming the first person to receive the prestigious Meilleur Ouvrier de France title, he co-founded Bar Pompette with two friends who joined him from France. Since then, he has helped guide the project to the city's highest ranking on North America's 50 Best Bars (2026) and the number one spot on Canada's 100 Best Bars (2024). Can you guess their signature drink? The answer might surprise you.**

What gap did you see in the Toronto bar scene that you wanted to fill with Pompette?

When I first arrived in Paris, you had hotel bars, a few historic institutions and maybe one or two standalone cocktail bars. I was working at the *Four Seasons Hotel George V* and later at *Le Bristol*. For a city that big, there wasn't a massive amount of high-quality variety. Around 2007, the *Experimental Cocktail Club* changed everything. That single bar incubated a whole generation of bartenders who went on to open their own spots.

Toronto felt like it was in a similar position to Paris, just ten years later. I realized this was our chance to not just participate in the evolution of the scene, but to be a real leader of that change. When we finally opened the bar, the concept was just a reflection of us. There wasn't a rigid concept beyond just being authentic to ourselves. But underneath it all, the ambition was to be Toronto's version of the Experimental Cocktail Club, to create a landmark space that would inspire many more great things to follow. That was the plan, even if we didn't explicitly spell it out at the start.

Your low-key approach to high-level technology has been described as "the Porsche in the garage." Do you agree with that description, and what's your favorite piece of tech?

When you work in high-end hotels, you constantly have to ask for permission, justify a budget, and deal with corporate red tape. When Jonathan [Bauer-Monneret], his wife [Martine Bauer] and I decided to open our place, we decided that everyone can buy what they want as long as we're going to use it. I bought a lot of cool tech to experiment more, but it's important that these technologies stay hidden. The guests who want to know about the tech can ask questions, but we love when people simply walk by the bar and say, "It looks cute, let's have a drink there" and then go, "Wow, the drinks are incredible."

When it comes to our equipment, we were the second bar in the city to get a Rotovap but perhaps the first to use it heavily. Today,

Photo: Jessica Blaine Smith

Bar Pompette
Little Italy

Bar Allegro
Little Italy

Trinity Bellwoods Park
Trinity Bellwoods

Toronto Islands
Lake Ontario

we have all the cool toys you could want. Over time, you realize that some are critical to your vision, while other tools that you underestimated turned out to be super versatile. Personally, I love to distill because it's so fun. Pardon my French, but I buy a whole bunch of shit just to distill it and see what the result is. You never know until you try. Sometimes you create terrible products, and sometimes you have total revelations. A few of our drinks are based on weird trials we did just out of curiosity.

What specific creation brings you the most pride?

The bar itself, honestly. But if I had to choose just one cocktail, I would say the Nitro Colada. It's funny because you can hold prestigious positions in Paris and travel the world, but when you open your own place, your best-selling drink turns out to be a piña colada!

We actually developed it during the pandemic. Because we couldn't sell open alcohol to-go, we had to make clarified milk punches and send them alongside a sealed bottle of alcohol. We did a whole bunch of experiments like that. One day, while shaking a milk punch, we realized that the fluffiness and creaminess we were getting from the texture would be absolutely incredible in a piña colada. We bought the very first nitro siphon that iSi had just launched, and we used it to develop a lighter version of the drink.

We use fresh pineapple juice and coconut water, and we fat-wash the rum with coconut oil. Then we add a house-made falernum infused with curry leaves. All of this goes right into the iSi nitro siphon. When you pour it, you get that beautiful cascading Guinness-style effect, along with all the fluffiness and creaminess you want from a traditional piña colada, but it's completely light. You can easily have two, three or four of them.

What are your other establishments right now?

We closed the restaurant at the end of 2025 to revamp the space and open a second bar called *Bar Allegro*. "Allegro" is the Italian

Sakai Bar
Brockton Village

Mhel
Dufferin Grove

Restaurant 20 Victoria
Financial District

Mother
Trinity Bellwoods

XXX
Fashion District

Blackbird Baking Co.
Various locations

Bellwoods Brewery
Various locations

Burdock Brewery
Various locations

Archive
Trinity Bellwoods

Cocktail Bar
Trinity Bellwoods

translation of Pompette, and "pompette" is the French word for being tipsy. We really wanted that name to describe the experience. It's a place where you go to loosen up and maybe have a little bit too much food or a little bit too much to drink. Our job is hospitality and trying to make people happy. We want people to enjoy life.

What are some of your favorite places to go in Toronto?

I live 30 kilometers away from the center, yet I'm still technically in Toronto, so my neighborhood has a totally different vibe. We have a park close to us called Trinity Bellwoods, which is a beautiful space where people go to unwind. We are located in the West End, which is considered the hipster part of the city, but it's super cool. You have tons of bars, restaurants and cafés, and the park sits right at the center of it all.

I also love the Toronto Islands. It's a fantastic place to completely disconnect. You take a 10-minute ferry ride and suddenly you are in the middle of nature, looking out at the lake. It's so quiet that you quickly forget you are still in Toronto with massive skyscrapers and millions of people right next to you.

In terms of food, *Sakai Bar* is a tiny Japanese spot on Dundas Street. The owner, Stuart, makes absolutely delicious food. There is also *Mhel*, a beautiful Korean-Japanese concept. Hoon, the chef, and his wife, Min, used to work with us. Hoon worked in our kitchen and Min led our coffee program back when Bar Pompette was open during the day.

If you are looking for local fine dining, I recommend *Restaurant 20 Victoria*. The chef, Rafa, is a good friend who visits us at the bar quite often. It's a small restaurant serving beautiful food. They have one Michelin star, but honestly, they could easily have two.

For bars, I like to go to *Mother*, and I'm a big martini person, so I love to head over to *XXX* to see the bartender, H. He's English, so he truly understands what a proper martini should be. He is a real character.

When it comes to bakeries, *Blackbird Baking Co.* is definitely a favorite. They started as a very small business and grew into multiple locations that supply bread to major hotels. Simon, one of the owners, is a neighbor of our restaurant and has been coming in since day one.

When you work in a bar and deal with cocktails all day long, sometimes you just crave a nice beer. We have two favorite local spots for that. First is *Bellwoods Brewery*. They make great local beers, especially sours and experimental styles. We also love *Burdock Brewery*. We created a collaboration beer with them called Spaltz, which is a nice Alsatian-style pilsner like the ones we love to drink back home. They have two locations: one in Kensington Market and one on Bloor Street.

For wine, *Archive* is a super cool, tiny wine bar. They have one of the best wine lists in the entire city. They are located a few doors down from us, which is amazing, but also a bit dangerous.

Finally, *Cocktail Bar* near us is owned by Jen Agg, one of the pioneers of independent bars and restaurants in Toronto. As a female entrepreneur, she had to fight incredibly hard to carve out a space for herself as an independent owner, and she is a real icon for a lot of people in this city. When it comes to cocktail bars, I just love her spaces so much. She has a real talent for creating gorgeous, thoughtful and deeply welcoming environments.

Captured Moments

One of Canada's leading galleries dedicated to photography, *Stephen Bulger Gallery* has been a fixture of the Dundas West gallery strip since the 1990s. The gallery represents major estates alongside leading contemporary photographers, and its inventory includes more than 30,000 prints spanning historical Canadian work and international modern photography. Exhibitions move between the documentary and the conceptual, giving equal weight to emerging photographers and figures who shaped the medium. The space also stocks an extensive selection of photography books, including rare and limited-edition titles.

• Stephen Bulger Gallery, 1356 Dundas Street West, Little Portugal, bulgergallery.com

Art & Design

Bricks to Brushstrokes

World-class museums share the same city streets with artist-run centers, photography archives, graffiti alleys and hidden works by Banksy. From Islamic masterpieces to Frank Gehry's final tower, Toronto treats art and design as something to be collected, challenged and reinvented.

Culture in Every Step

North America's only museum dedicated to the history and cultural significance of footwear, the *Bata Shoe Museum* was born from Sonja Bata's personal collection, assembled over decades of travel alongside her husband's global shoe empire. The collection now spans more than 15,000 objects dating back 4,500 years, from ancient Egyptian sandals and Indigenous North American moccasins to Queen Victoria's ballroom slippers and Elton John's platforms. Raymond Moriyama designed the building as a giant shoebox, its angled limestone facade and tilted roof suggesting a lid resting just slightly askew.

• Bata Shoe Museum, 327 Bloor Street West, The Annex, batashoemuseum.ca

Photos: Destination Canada, Scott Poborsa / Guillaume Simoneau *Murder* (2020)

Future Voices

If you want to see what Toronto's next generation of artists is making, *Xpace Cultural Centre* is the place. The artist-run spot is supported by the OCAD Student Union but operates independently, giving emerging and student practitioners a professional platform across multiple spaces. Collaborating with curators like TRIPTYCH (photo), the programming leans experimental, with exhibitions, panels and workshops that treat art-making as a form of world-building and prioritize marginalized, racialized, Black and Indigenous artists.

• Xpace Cultural Centre, 303 Lansdowne Avenue, Unit 2, Brockton Village, xpace.info

The Idea Factory

Near the corner of Spadina and Richmond, *401 Richmond* is the largest hub of its kind in Toronto, packing more than 140 creative spaces across four floors. Originally a tin lithography factory, the building sat empty for decades until Margaret Zeidler bought and renovated it in 1994, preserving the original brick and wood. The main floor alone holds 10 galleries, while artist studios, print shops and project spaces fill the floors above. At its center, a hidden courtyard offers a quiet break from all that creative density.

• 401 Richmond, 401 Richmond Street West, Fashion District, 401richmond.com

Photo: Alison [illegible]/TRIPTYCH

Photo: Toni Hafkenscheid, The Image Centre, 2026

The World in Frames

The Image Centre is a leading institution dedicated entirely to photography and lens-based media. It was built around the Black Star Collection, an archive of nearly 300,000 images donated to Toronto Metropolitan University by the famed New York photo agency in 2005 and housed at the center. Assembled over eight decades by more than 6,000 photographers who documented the 20th century in its full breadth and complexity, the collection now includes the archives of Berenice Abbott, Wendy Snyder MacNeil and Jo Spence, with an exhibition program that matches the collection's ambition.

• **The Image Centre, 33 Gould Street, Garden District, theimagecentre.ca**

Echoes of Empire

The only museum in North America dedicated to Islamic art and culture, the *Aga Khan Museum* spans medieval Persia and Mughal India to the present-day Muslim world. Its collection traces 14 centuries of scientific and artistic achievement, from illuminated manuscripts and astronomical instruments to ceramics, textiles and courtly paintings. The building, designed by Pritzker Prize–winning architect Fumihiko Maki, is as much a draw as the art. Conceived around the idea of light, it has angled granite facades that shift with the sun, while inside, hexagonal skylights and mashrabiya-patterned courtyard walls cast shifting patterns across white stone.

- Aga Khan Museum, 77 Wynford Drive, North York, agakhanmuseum.org

Finding Banksy

It may seem silly to go wandering through a corporate building in downtown Toronto searching for famous art. But it's no joke. Follow the PATH to One York and go to the second floor to see Banksy's 2010 piece *Security Guard with Pink Balloon Dog* carefully excavated from its original location and preserved behind plexiglass. Down the hallway? Toronto's Second City comedy club. The piece is one of two surviving Banksy pieces in Toronto. The other, smaller piece, *Men Onlooking* (photo), lives close by, tucked down an alleyway in the Esplanade.

- Various locations

Legacy of the Lens

Opening her gallery in 1979 at a time when few Canadians took photo art seriously, Jane Corkin spent decades changing that perception, spotlighting image makers like Diane Arbus, Robert Mapplethorpe and André Kertész along the way. The gallery now occupies a converted tank house in the Distillery District with enough space to run several exhibitions simultaneously. It maintains a significant collection of historical photography alongside a roster of emerging and mid-career contemporary artists working across photography, painting, sculpture and installation

• Corkin Gallery, 7 Tank House Lane, Distillery District, corkingallery.com

Rush the Walls

Rush Lane runs three blocks through the Fashion District, its walls covered floor to ceiling in murals and tags. What's now one of Toronto's most photographed stretches started as unsanctioned graffiti, until local business owners pushed back against property fines in 2011 and the city designated the alley an area of municipal significance. The move launched StreetARToronto, the program that now funds public murals across the city. Artists including Uber5000, Elicser and Spud have left work here, and the alley stays in constant flux, with new pieces appearing and old ones painted over, so no two visits look the same.

• Rush Lane (Graffiti Alley), between Spadina Avenue and Portland Street, south of Queen Street West

Photos: Erman Gunes, Christian Butterfield's *Green Light* (Corkin Gallery)

Canada's Art Canon

Since 1900, Toronto's premier art institution has been building a strong permanent collection that now spans more than 120,000 works. Frank Gehry's 2008 redesign wrapped the AGO building in a spiraling wood staircase and a sweeping glass facade that floods the interior with light, making the architecture worth the visit alone. The redesign added more than 47,000 square feet of gallery space and introduced the Walker Court, a soaring atrium at the heart of the building that now hosts major installations, events, and a regular program of performances, talks, and film screenings tied to the exhibitions on view.

The eclectic holdings range from Group of Seven canvases that shaped how Canadians see their own landscape to the world's largest public collection of works by British artist Henry Moore, as well as Indigenous art, African art, European masters, and a Yayoi Kusama Infinity Mirrored Room. The exhibition program has a strong record of presenting major international traveling shows alongside survey exhibitions of both canonical and underrepresented artists, with past highlights including Frida Kahlo, Jean-Michel Basquiat, and Michelangelo. A seventh expansion is currently underway to increase space for the growing modern and contemporary collection.

• Art Gallery of Ontario, 317 Dundas Street West, Grange Park, ago.ca

Frank Gehry Comes Home

Frank Gehry, one of the world's most celebrated architects, was born in Toronto in 1929 to Polish immigrant parents. His earliest creative influence is often said to have been his grandmother, who scattered odd-shaped wood scraps across her kitchen floor and encouraged the young Gehry to build imaginary cities before the pieces were tossed into the stove. After moving to Los Angeles as a teenager, he went on to redefine contemporary architecture on a global scale.

Among his best-known works are the Guggenheim Museum Bilbao, Walt Disney Concert Hall in Los Angeles and Fondation Louis Vuitton in Paris. Yet Toronto, the city where it all began, is home to two significant Gehry projects.

The first is the *Art Gallery of Ontario*. Completed in 2008, the redesign marked Gehry's first major commission in Canada and a return to the place where he first connected art and architecture. His transformation opened the institution to the city through a sweeping glass facade along Dundas Street and new public-facing gallery spaces. The Allan Slaight and Emmanuelle Gattuso Spiral Staircase (photo) remains one of the gallery's defining features.

His last major Toronto project, *Forma*, is currently rising on King Street West. The pair of mixed-use towers, set to reach 73 and 84 stories, will feature sculptural facades that fold and ripple. Gehry described Forma as his most personal project, a return to the city of his birth. When completed, the buildings will be the tallest Gehry development in the world and among Canada's tallest towers. The East Tower is slated for completion as early as 2028, while the West Tower doesn't have a start date. Gehry passed away in December 2025 at the age of 96.

• Gehry Partners, foga.com

Bareket Kezwer

In Living Color

Bareket Kezwer is a Toronto-based muralist whose signature rainbow geometry and bold typography can be found on walls across the city, from hospital corridors to alleyways in Parkdale and Kensington Market. In 2017, she founded Women Paint, a street-art initiative that has since produced more than 100 murals by women, nonbinary and gender nonconforming artists. Her practice is rooted in a belief that color has the power to transform urban space and that public art belongs to everyone.

Your work combines bold geometry, color and typography in a way that's immediately recognizable. How did that visual language develop?

It developed through experiences in my life. I studied graphic design, so a lot of it is informed by that. I also did four years of visual language training. And then there's my own personal aesthetic: I'm drawn to bright colors and bold visual language, and that seems to be what flows through me.

You describe color as medicine. Can you tell us more about this idea?

I spend a lot of time thinking about the urban environments we move through, and they're so often gray and beige and muted. The natural world has so many colors in it, particularly here, living in a country with four seasons. Spring, summer and fall are all incredibly colorful, and then winter is more muted, and I think so many people feel that as we emerge from winter, the colors of spring really help us feel a sense of coming back to life. In the same way that flowers use color to attract pollinators, color is something that helps us connect with that feeling of being alive, of vibrancy, of health and vitality. Color speaks to a certain part of our soul and helps us remember warmth and beauty. Within the context of our gray, muted cities, it can help us remember that there is more than what can sometimes feel like oppressive structures. There are spaces for beauty, for joy, for spontaneity, connection, playfulness, curiosity and growth.

You founded Women Paint in 2017. What was the impulse behind it?

It grew out of a particular moment when a lot was happening in the world that felt complicated and politically charged. I noticed that within my own work environment, so many of the spaces I found myself in were heavily dominated by men. Yet I personally knew so many incredibly talented female painters. I wanted to create a space where we could get together, support each other, build community and share our stories. The reality that so many of those spaces were male-dominated meant that much more of the public art I was seeing came from a male perspective. It felt really important to add more female narratives to the streets. If we're 50 percent of the population, it's important that our voices are present in daily life.

How has it evolved over time?

I run five events through Women Paint, and they've grown in complexity and scale, and also in terms of nuance. When I first started, I was really thinking about women, but as it evolved, I started thinking more about the broader community of gender-diverse people: women, nonbinary folks, trans folks, folks who don't fit into neat categories. Another big part of the project that evolved was mentorship, creating opportunities for emerging artists to gain experience by being mentored by more established ones. We also introduced a camp for youth, giving a group of young people the opportunity to learn about mural painting, collaboratively design their own mural and then paint it together. It's so important that young people have the opportunity to add their voices to the street. So much of our world prioritizes adult voices, and young people have a huge amount to contribute to public discourse.

Many of your murals are made together with the communities they're for. How does that process work?

The process is different every time. It's really about getting to know the community, and that looks different depending on who they are. I make space to listen, to understand what's important to them, what they would want to see in their space, the stories they want to share with their community and with the wider city. I also try to understand what symbols are meaningful to them and how to create artwork that represents their voices. That often creates an opportunity for people to participate in the co-creation directly, through workshops where people make visual art, poetry or storytelling, and the work created in those workshops often appears within the mural itself.

How would you describe Toronto's street-art scene right now?

It's really vibrant and diverse, and it's growing. There's a conscious effort to include new

Kensington Market
Kensington Market

Graffiti Alley
Fashion District

Dundas West
West Queen West

History
Upper Beach

Longboat Hall
West Queen West

voices, and it feels like a space of constant evolution.

Which parts of the city have the most interesting walls?

Kensington Market has incredible art that's always changing. *Graffiti Alley* is amazing. And honestly, so many of the laneways all over the city have incredible work. *Dundas West* is another area with really strong murals. The art is everywhere.

Any artists we should be keeping an eye on?

There are so many incredible artists in this city. Caitlin Taguibao, Ryan Dineen, June Kim, Ghazaleh Rastgar, Nick Sweetman, Elicser, Julia Prajza, Chris Perez, Moises Frank, Jacquie Comrie, Melika Saeeda, Emily May Rose, Christina Mazzulla and Phillip Saunders, to name a few.

What are the art and cultural spaces you find essential in Toronto?

I'm really into live music. There are so many great venues in the city. I go to a lot of shows at *History*, and there's an incredible music series called Listening Room at *Longboat Hall* that I absolutely love. There's also a really vibrant dance community in Toronto. I love

Isza Gallery
St. Lawrence Market

Worth Gallery
Trinity Bellwoods

Mattachioni
The Junction

Loga's Corner
Parkdale

Dear Grain
Various locations

High Park
High Park North

Toronto Islands
Lake Ontario

Ecstatic Dance Toronto and the rave scene, which takes over different spaces around the city.

And there are some incredible galleries all over the city, including several specifically focused on street and urban art that are doing really strong shows. One is *Isza Gallery* on King Street East near Church, and another is *Worth Gallery* on Dundas Street.

What are your favorite spots to eat in Toronto, places that feel like home?

I eat a lot at *Mattachioni*, a little Italian place close to my house with amazing sourdough bread, pizza and sandwiches. I also love *Loga's Corner*, a Tibetan momo spot that I keep going back to. My favorite bakery is *Dear Grain*. I love wandering around different neighborhoods and trying whatever I find, whether that's dumplings in Chinatown or something completely new. Toronto has a really vibrant food culture.

How do you spend a day off in the city?

I often go to *High Park*. I love wandering around there. It's huge and gorgeous, and you feel almost outside of the city while still being in it. I also really love walking along the waterfront. And I love going to *Toronto Islands*, which have that same quality of feeling removed from the city, with this incredible view of the skyline from the water.

Where do you go when you want to briefly escape Toronto?

My friends have cottages in Muskoka, which is a beautiful escape. And there are amazing waterfall hikes in Hamilton that I really love.

Book-Smart Design

From brutalist monoliths to light-filled atriums, Toronto's schools and libraries turn everyday learning into a study in architectural style.

The Glass Library

From the outside, the *Toronto Reference Library*, a terraced brick building designed by Raymond Moriyama in the 1970s, looks almost deliberately understated, blending into the neighborhood rather than dominating it. Inside it tells a different story. The building opens onto a vast tiered atrium inspired by the Hanging Gardens of Babylon and a skylight flooding the space with natural light. A 2010s renovation added a glowing glass entrance cube, a freestanding theater, a 600-seat literary salon and a rotunda for special collections in concrete, titanium and dark wood.

• Toronto Reference Library, 789 Yonge Street, Bloor-Yorkville, tpl.ca

Photo: Steven Kriemadis

Stainless Style

Across from the AGO, the *Rosalie Sharp Pavilion* is wrapped in a stainless-steel scrim with a laser-cut pattern based on an art map of Toronto, with its perforations marking galleries, studios and public art spaces. The scrim's edges curl upward and outward, echoing the curves of Frank Gehry's AGO facade and catching the light differently throughout the day. Inside, the renovated building houses OCAD University's Experiential Learning Centre and the RBC Centre for Emerging Artists and Designers, with studio space and exhibitions open to visitors.

• Rosalie Sharp Pavilion, OCAD University, 115 McCaul Street, Grange Park, ocadu.ca

Concrete Knowledge

Robarts Library opened in 1973 as the largest academic library in the world, its raw concrete, triangular tower and hexagonal wings earning it the nickname Fort Book. Opinions have been divided ever since, with the building called both a brutalist masterpiece and one of the city's biggest eyesores. From outside, it presents a stark, fortress-like silhouette, while inside, narrow stacks, low ceilings and a maze of concrete stairwells give it its labyrinthine reputation. In 2022, Diamond Schmitt Architects added Robarts Common, a glass-walled extension whose angular form nods to the original's geometry.

• Robarts Library, 130 St. George Street, The Annex, library.utoronto.ca/library/robarts

A Photo Showcase

Reframing the Archive

by Christina Leslie

DEH'YA FEST
CAT

Christina Leslie is a Toronto-based artist whose lens-based practice explores decolonization, identity, migration and her West Indian heritage through experimental photography. Working with historical photographic processes and unconventional materials, including pinhole cameras and sugar as a photographic medium, she builds what she calls a fake archive, a visual record of Black diasporic histories that was never made but should have been.

Your practice draws on your West Indian heritage to explore histories of colonialism, migration and diaspora, stories that have often been suppressed or erased. What draws you to those historical gaps?

Being a biracial woman, I noticed during my BFA that the artists referenced in my studies rarely reflected stories concerning the diaspora. There was a white-centric sharing of knowledge, and I don't mean that pejoratively. That's just the reality. Other knowledges, other stories, other narratives were relegated to a footnote or rarely shared at all. My lived experience wasn't reflected in the materials we were shown, and when I looked further into the archives and the broader canon of art history, there were just so many gaps. I kept asking myself: How can I insert myself to create some kind of presence?

Over 20 years ago, the disparity was enormous, and that became my motivating factor. As I kept creating work and doing more research, it just kept pulling me in. I see myself as having a responsibility to share other perspectives, especially those of marginalized voices.

Your series Sugar Coat *uses physical sugar as a photographic material, referencing the history of the Caribbean sugar trade. How did you arrive at using the material to carry that history?*

I was thinking about the labor of hands behind the cultivation of sugar. Why

wouldn't I then create a series that in some way replicated that process, even if just in its tediousness? That history is also very violent, so I wanted to pay some kind of homage to the labor involved in making these photographs. I also didn't want sugar to appear in the photograph in a tame way, like a bag of sugar on a shelf. I thought, wouldn't it be more interesting to actually make the photograph out of sugar? Because sugar is something we consume, and we consume history all the time.

The technique took me about four years to nail down, and I'd like to patent it eventually, just because of how long it took to develop. What's interesting is that the sugar pieces become objects. The photographs are already objects, but these images are also physically fragile. Some have broken in the process of perfecting the technique, and I think that speaks to history as well. Everything ties into each other.

You also work extensively with pinhole photography, making your own lenses and cameras. Can you walk us through how it works and what this historical process brings to the work?

Photography has its origins in the camera obscura, and from its earliest stages, the medium has been used to surveil and categorize marginalized people, to perpetuate stereotypes. The Black body and the Black diaspora were rarely photographed on their own terms. When you look at early photographic history, the images of Black people were largely framed around slavery: auction blocks, the famous photograph of the man with the flagellated back, the circulation of Frederick Douglass's image by abolitionists. We were not owners of our own images.

That history is why I should use something like the pinhole camera. I wanted to reference the early history of photography while creating images as if a Black diasporic archive had always existed, even though it doesn't. It's almost a fake archive. If those images had existed, this is what they might have looked like.

A pinhole camera is essentially a light-tight box with a tiny hole that lets light pass through onto a piece of photographic film inside, projecting an image. Instead of making a camera out of a shoebox, I convert my digital camera into a pinhole camera by making my own lenses, using pins of different sizes to create different apertures and different effects. I've even used an earring backing as a pin. When I'm traveling, I make the lenses from materials I find in the city. In New York, I used foil, tape and a water bottle. I even used a tea bag once to soften the image and create graininess.

For the Toronto photographs, I went to the Caribbean Carnival, which used to be called Caribana, with two cameras. I wanted to photograph it with the pinhole, thinking: What if we had early archival images of the carnival? What would they look like? So I went with my DSLR for documentary shots and did something more artistic with the pinhole.

sandro
Abercrombie
& Fitch
NOW OPEN

Shops

Retail Remedies

From heritage markets and vinyl bins to design-forward concept stores, Toronto's retail scene is built on discovery, not just consumption.

New to You

Vancouverite Courtney Watkins opened the Toronto outpost of her boutique consignment store, *Mine & Yours*, in 2023. It's one of three locations in the country, and the only one in Eastern Canada, meaning this is the spot to shop for your Valentino mini-dress, Gucci handbag or red-bottomed heels (especially if you love a deal). The Yorkville store offers rigorously curated secondhand luxury goods, including clothing, shoes, jewelry and other accessories. The color-coded wall of totes, slings and everything in between is a bag buff's dream.

- Mine & Yours, 79 Yorkville Avenue, Yorkville, mineandyours.com

Literary Misfits

Named after W. W. Jacobs's horror story, the *Monkey's Paw* specializes in books too strange for ordinary categories: tales of medical oddities, forgotten manuals and titles on subjects so niche you'd be surprised anyone wrote a book about them. One of the store's most beloved attractions is the Biblio-mat, a hulking green-and-ivory vending machine built in 2012 but designed to look like something from the 1940s. The first machine of its kind, it dispenses a random vintage book for the price of a token, turning the simple act of buying a book into a small gamble.

• The Monkey's Paw, 1067 Bloor Street West, Dufferin Grove, monkeyspaw.com

The Beat Goes On

The Ossington-Dundas strip, one of Toronto's most popular destinations for both tourists and locals, has undergone many iterations over the last few years. Despite these changes, there are still excellent hole-in-the-wall and independent stores peppered among the generic chains. *Rotate This*, a stalwart of the Toronto record scene, sits just south of Dundas. The shop specializes in both new and used records, with vinyl that stretches as far and as high as the eye can see. With its diverse selection and knowledgeable staff, it's beyond a must-visit for any music lover.

• Rotate This, 186 Ossington Avenue, Ossington Village, @rotatethis

Skate, Sip, Share

Brockton Haunt is a coffee shop, skate hub and community space that draws a diverse and inclusive crowd. The shop is also fully licensed, mostly serving canned drinks like beers and ciders. On special nights, it's packed to the rafters for comedy shows, acoustic music sets and screenings. A neighborhood fixture for more than a decade, the woman-owned shop is widely embraced as a welcoming space for the LGBTQ+ community. It operates as a true third space where culture, conversation and caffeine intersect.

• Brockton Haunt, 1158 College Street, Dufferin Grove, brocktonhaunt.ca

Photos: Vanessa Webster, Marko Djurdjic

Containing Community

One of the most architecturally unique spaces in the city, Toronto's *STACKT Market* is a flexible, community-driven development that merges commerce and retail with the human need for connection. Built primarily from shipping containers, STACKT shifts with every season, rotating brands, events, art and public spaces. There are pickleball and basketball courts, curling lanes and plenty of dog-friendly green space. It's fully accessible and open year-round. Whether you're looking for a crisp beer or a conversation with a stranger, STACKT is an urban playground for the adventurous adult.

- STACKT Market, 28 Bathurst Street, West Queen West, stacktmarket.com

Treasure Hunting

Toronto is a multicultural city, and nowhere is that more apparent than in *Kensington Market*, a bustling microvillage in Toronto's West End that's got a little bit of everything. Think vintage shops with fantastic finds from across the decades, cuisine from every corner of the globe, public murals and art spanning different genres, and breweries and bars that transform into performance halls and event spaces. In the summer, pedestrian-only streets help accommodate the crowds. Everywhere you look, Kensington Market is alive with color, sound, people and discoveries waiting to happen.

- Kensington Market, Downtown West, @kensingtonmarketbia

The Artist Archive

Founded in 1974 by the artist collective General Idea, *Art Metropole* takes its name from a defunct gallery that once occupied the same building. It's now the oldest artist-run bookstore in the world, stocking more than 16,000 artists' books, multiples, zines and other publications that rarely surface through mainstream channels, with a particular focus on inclusive creators. After decades of moving between Toronto addresses, it landed on College Street in 2021, where its modular shelving, designed by artist Christian Kliegel, can be reconfigured for book launches, panel discussions and other events.

• Art Metropole, 896 College Street, Little Italy, artmetropole.com

The First Market

Toronto's oldest operating market first opened to the public in 1803 as a small, open-air destination for commerce and trade. Today, *St. Lawrence Market* is a sprawling, three-building complex with multiple stories and hundreds of vendors throughout the week. The South Market is open most of the week, offering local favorites such as St. Urbain Bagel Bakery, Kozlik's Canadian Mustard and Carousel Bakery, famous for its peameal bacon sandwich. Meanwhile, the Farmer's and North Markets are only open Saturdays, with a vintage market taking over the big white tent every Sunday.

• St. Lawrence Market, 92-95 Front Street East, St. Lawrence, stlawrencemarket.com

Sunday Digs

A Sunday exclusive, the *West End Market* features eclectic wares from a wide variety of local vendors. It's a true flea market, with affordable prices and some room to barter on everything from vintage clothing and antique furniture to fresh pastries and custom art. The vendors rotate regularly, with some popping up for only a week at a time, so it's worth making return visits to see what new treasures await discovery. Fuel up with a coffee from the steampunk-themed Atlantis Steamworks café and then dive in. There's a lot to peruse.

• The West End Market, 1605 Queen Street West, The Parkdale Hall, Parkdale, theparkdalehall.com

Photos: Daniel Neuhaus, Toronto Sunday Market/The Parkdale Hall, Destination Canada

Toronto Together

From street and beach parties to design and art festivals, the cultural calendar is always in motion. These are the moments where the city comes together in real time.

The City in Focus

In 1997, gallery owner Stephen Bulger put out a call asking who in Toronto had wall space to exhibit photographs for a few weeks. The response was bigger than anyone expected and gave rise to *CONTACT*, now one of the largest photography festivals in the world. Major museums and galleries anchor the spring program—with Gagné Contemporary Projects exhibiting the 2026 In Transit series by Mathew Merrett (photo)—but anyone can register a show in a storefront, subway station or other public space and become an official part of the festival.

• CONTACT Photography Festival, various locations, contactphoto.com

Winter by Design

Every January, *DesignTO* turns the depths of winter into Toronto's busiest season for design, with more than a hundred exhibitions, installations and talks spread across galleries, shops, lobbies and studios. Exhibitions span furniture, fashion, architecture and product design, often staged in spaces that aren't normally open to the public. One highlight is Come Up to My Room at the Gladstone House, where designers take over individual hotel rooms for a few days, transforming them into experimental installations somewhere between showroom and art piece.

• DesignTO Festival, various locations, designto.org

Photo: Mathew Merrett @mephotomat

Photo: Destination Canada

Carnival on the Lake

Every August, the *Toronto Caribbean Carnival* transforms Lakeshore Boulevard into one of the most spectacular parades in North America. Known to most Torontonians as Caribana, the festival has been a fixture of Toronto summers since 1967, spanning three weeks of parties, concerts and cultural events, with the Grand Parade on Emancipation Day weekend as its centerpiece. More than a million spectators line the 2.2-mile route, watching Mas bands pass in elaborate feathered and rhinestoned costumes, to the sound of soca, calypso and steel pan bands filling the waterfront.

- Toronto Caribbean Carnival, Lakeshore Boulevard, Fort York, torontocarnival.ca

Summary Stages

For nearly two weeks in early July, the *Toronto Fringe Festival* brings more than a hundred theater productions to dozens of local venues. Programming is selected by lottery, so it's usually a very diverse agenda that spans dramas, stand-up comedy, musicals, dance, children's theater, performance art and beyond. Of course, this means not all the shows are amazing, which is why festival-goers, colloquially known as Fringers, adore trading recommendations over drinks at the Festival Hub in the Distillery District. Many shows have pick-your-price options starting in the single digits, so why not take a chance?

• Toronto Fringe Festival, various locations, fringetoronto.com

The Rave Underground

Pep Rally started in 2019 when DJs Chippy Nonstop and Karim Olen Ash decided Toronto needed a rave built specifically for queer, BIPOC and women partygoers who didn't always feel at home in the city's existing club scene. It's grown into one of the city's most talked-about underground parties, with sold-out themed nights held in warehouses and industrial spaces—and the occasional secret outdoor summer event, location often revealed only days before. Expect international guest DJs, elaborate outfits and a crowd for whom getting dressed up is its own kind of performance.

• Pep Rally, various locations, @itspeprally

Photo: Colleen Yates

Floating Lights

Held each September at Downsview Park, the *Toronto Water Lantern Festival* invites participants to decorate eco-friendly floating lanterns with messages, artwork, wishes or tributes before releasing them onto the water at sunset. As darkness settles in, hundreds of glowing lanterns drift across the lake's surface, creating one of the city's most enchanting autumn spectacles. Food trucks, live music and community activities add to the atmosphere, while the collective lantern launch offers a moment of reflection, hope and connection.

• Water Lantern Festival, Downsview Park, 70 Canuck Avenue, North York, waterlanternfestival.com

Cherry Beach Sessions

Every Sunday from June through Labour Day, *Promise Cherry Beach* takes over the sandy shore of Cherry Beach Park for an afternoon dance party that's been a cornerstone of Toronto's underground electronic music scene since 2000. Played on a Funktion One sound system, the music leans house, techno, disco and electro, drawing occasional surprise visits from international guests. All ages are welcome, there's a licensed beach bar on-site, and the vibe sits somewhere between underground rave and neighborhood hangout, with picnic blankets spread across the sand alongside people dancing until sunset.

• Promise Cherry Beach, Cherry Beach Park, Port Lands, promisecherrybeach.com

Get lost in the right places
OPEN
Off the map, but in your feed. Follow for hard-to-find recommendations.

Outdoors

Wild in the City

From island beaches and forested trails to lakeside parks just minutes from downtown, Toronto's outdoors feels surprisingly vast. These are the spots where water, wilderness and skyline meet.

Photo: Destination Toronto

Call Your Bluff

The far-east district of Scarborough covers roughly 30 percent of Toronto's land area, and there are some gorgeous spots along the water. Most notable is the Scarborough Bluffs, a nine-mile stretch of cliffs, trails, beaches and gardens split across 11 parks offering different vantage points. To tackle this mammoth area, the best approach is to start at Bluffer's Park, which has access to great views, and then explore further as time permits. If you're driving and it's a summer weekend, arrive nice and early: The parking lot fills up quickly.

- Bluffer's Park, 1 Brimley Road South, Scarborough

Photo: Erman Gunes/Shutterstock.com

Beach Tour

The beaches on the Toronto Islands each have their own atmosphere. To the east is Ward's Island Beach, a tranquil location with cottage-country vibes. Centre Island Beach is closest to its namesake attraction, *Centreville Amusement Park*, boasting concessions, locker rooms and a splash pad for family-friendly fun. Hidden behind a lighthouse to the southwest is the quiet shore of Gibraltar Point Beach. Finally, dominating the western edge of the islands is Hanlan's Point, Canada's oldest queer social space and clothing-optional beach. Come for the islands, stay for the beaches.

• Various locations, torontoisland.com/beach.php

Pool Party Central

Perched on Toronto's waterfront at Polson Pier, with uninterrupted views of the city skyline, Cabana brings a distinctly Miami-style energy to the edge of Lake Ontario. Part beach club, part outdoor entertainment venue, it revolves around a sprawling pool deck lined with loungers, private cabanas and bars serving frozen cocktails throughout the day. During summer, the space hosts DJs, parties and live events, drawing a crowd looking to make the most of the short Canadian warm season. Arrive early for a laid-back afternoon in the sun or stay as the atmosphere shifts into full weekend-party mode.

- Cabana Pool Bar, 11 Polson Street, Polson Pier, cabanatoronto.com

Urban Hiking

A former industrial site and quarry located in the Don River Valley, *Evergreen Brick Works* is now a community hub and public events space. Food markets, gardens, a community events space and 1.5 miles of beautiful walking trails make it a family-friendly destination with plenty of activities. The space is accessible by car, transit or bike, but the most exciting way to reach the lushly forested ravine is on foot. There are multiple access points and trails with varying levels of difficulty. Choose your own adventure to reach the destination.

- Evergreen Brick Works, 550 Bayview Avenue, Don Valley, evergreen.ca/evergreen-brick-works

Photos: Destination Canada, V. L. CC 1.0

Bite of the Wild

If you need a break from the city, there's no better place for a breath of fresh air than the ominously named *Rattlesnake Point* in the Niagara Escarpment, a short train ride or drive from the city center. The sheer limestone cliffs draw rock climbers as the equally ominous turkey vultures circle overhead like winged opportunists. With tent-friendly campsites and more than 60 miles of hiking trails snaking through a dense forest of ancient cedars, this stunning conservation area is the perfect place to take in Ontario's beautiful biodiversity. Follow the trails to panoramic escarpment views, where the city feels a world away and the only traffic overhead comes with wings.

- Rattlesnake Point Conservation Area, 7200 Appleby Line, Milton, ontarioconservationareas.ca

Photo: tigerstrawberry

Idyllic Evenings

Riverdale Park East is the spot that justifies Broadview Avenue's name. A large, wide grassy hill, it offers one of the best non-island views of Toronto's skyline. During the city's few months of warm weather, sunsets on the hill become a massive community event, with locals throwing down blankets and munching on takeout from nearby Greektown or East Chinatown. Inevitably, someone queues up chill music on a speaker as groups of friends play Frisbee and volleyball. Who says Toronto is only about the grindset?

- Riverdale Park East, 550 Broadview Avenue

Lakeside Trails

Lake Ontario can take a long time to access on public transit, but thanks to *Tommy Thompson Park* (a.k.a. the Leslie Street Spit), bikers have it easier. This car-free peninsula protrudes about three miles into the lake, hosting 1,200 acres of urban wilderness. There's a BikeShare rack right at the spit's entrance. You're also allowed to hike or rollerblade. Despite the park's human-made origins, there's tons of wildlife, including birds like eagles, herons and egrets. Keep going toward the tip for sweeping lake views and a spectacular look back at Toronto's skyline, which feels surprisingly distant from this reclaimed slice of wilderness. Make sure to confirm the atypical hours: The park is usually closed before 4pm on weekdays.

- Tommy Thompson Park, 1 Leslie Street, Port Lands, tommythompsonpark.ca

Photos: Destination Toronto, Keylight Studio

Ledge Hunters

Toronto rarely tops the list of North America's most celebrated skate cities, but that's part of its appeal. Beneath the radar lies a city packed with skate shops, DIY parks and iconic street spots that reward those willing to explore.

Before you hit the parks and street spots, hit up one of the local skate shops, many of which are independently owned. *So Hip Toronto* is a staple, but *Blue Tile Lounge* is the GOAT. For more than 20 years, the Queen West institution has served as a clubhouse for the skate community, with carefully curated gear, skate videos running all day and staff who seem to know everyone worth knowing. If you're new to the scene, go to one of these shops, ask questions and show you care, and you'll get the scoop.

Lucas, one of Blue Tile's most recognizable employees, describes the Toronto skate scene as a community-based endeavor. "Having what we have here is really special," he says. "Every time you go to any park, you run into somebody you know, you skate with them, and there is no animosity between anyone in the city. It's too small for that!"

Dylan, a frequent patron of the shop, says he "made all [his] good friends through skateboarding," and that "various spots in the city cater to various skill levels, regardless of where you're coming from." For beginners, he recommends *Christie Pits* skatepark, which self-identifies as "Toronto's first concrete skatepark downtown and the first legal-ish DIY in the city." He describes it as "a great DIY park. It's a younger crowd with a mellow vibe, and any skill level can go there."

Ben, another employee, loves the Toronto skate scene because "the community out here is strong, and everyone sticks together. It's not cliquey," which is essential when visiting a new skate city without a direct entry point. "There are so many places to skate in Toronto that it's hard to see all of it," he continues. "Often, you just end up by the water after skating and chill and have a couple of pints."

While Toronto has numerous free spots peppered around the city like *Ashbridge Bay Skatepark*, it's essential that any skater worth their trucks hit up some of the more famous non-designated skate spots, most of which have appeared in your favorite skate videos featuring Toronto. These locales might not be "permissible" skate spots, but here we go: the plazas around the CBC headquarters; the SkyDome 13 stairs near the Rogers Centre; HTO Park; and Roy Thomson Hall, a concert venue with skateable ledges, stairs and rails. There's also the University of Toronto campus, about which Ben warns, "Security might be on your ass, but it's nice."

The local skate scene is so dedicated that there is even a School Board–sanctioned alternative high school, *Oasis Skateboard Factory*, which offers students an opportunity to earn high school credits by engaging with the curriculum through skateboarding. While it isn't accessible to the public (it is a school, after all), it is located right next to *Dunbat*, a skater-built and -funded park that has been operating since 2003. It's also one of the most accessible and visitor-friendly spots in the city. Blue Tile Lounge even did a project with Oasis where students designed custom-made grip tape that was sold at the shop, with all profits going to the kids.

• Various locations

Photo: Destination Toronto

Island Escape

The Toronto Islands consist of 15 interconnected islands south of the mainland. Round-trip-only public ferries depart from Jack Layton Ferry Terminal all year long, while seasonal, privately owned water taxis shuttle passengers seeking a more intimate, often themed experience. The ferries dock at Centre Island, Ward's Island and Hanlan's Point, so make sure you board the one that brings you closest to your desired destination.

The Island, as locals call it, is bike-friendly, with personal bikes permitted on the ferries and several *Bike Share Toronto* docking stands located at various points. *Toronto Island Bicycle Rental* even offers tandems and quadricycles. There are plenty of water sports options, including rentable stand-up paddleboards, as well as numerous playgrounds and green spaces for recreation, picnicking and exploring. *Toronto Island Park Disc Golf Course*—a world-class, no-charge, first-come, first-served 18-hole course—is set on Ward's Island, while Centreville, an amusement park that has been operating for 50-plus years, features more than 30 rides and attractions for different ages and bravery levels, including an antique horse carousel, roller coasters, an interactive farm and a gondola that offers aerial views of the park.

There are boardwalks, winding paths and lookout points all over, including Centre Island Pier and the Gibraltar Point Lighthouse. If you love a lil' noise with your strolls, the Island also hosts concerts and events. Electric Island, a series of open-air weekend festivals, happens throughout the spring and summer, while Upper Deck Bar couples live music, karaoke, trivia and bingo nights with incredible views of the Toronto skyline.

Hanlan's Point Beach is Canada's oldest surviving queer space. It's clothing optional, so keep that in mind when packing your swimsuit—or not. If you prefer to sweat indoors, a sauna facility opening in 2027 will convert a decommissioned fire station into a place to lounge and recharge, maintaining the Island's tradition of repurposing old spaces into new ones.

And remember, while the Islands offer fun and leisure for all visitors, more than 600 residents call them home, so be respectful.

- Toronto Islands, torontoisland.com

Be an elite diner
Earn 2X points on gas station, grocery store and dining purchases
The Air Canada Aeroplan® Card
Experience something elite.
Learn more at Chase.com/AirCanadaCard
AIR CANADA AEROPLAN
CHASE
Mastercard, the circles design, World Mastercard and World Elite Mastercard are trademarks of Mastercard International Incorporated. Chase Air Canada Aeroplan Card credit cards are issued by JPMorgan Chase Bank, N.A. Member FDIC. Accounts subject to credit approval. Restrictions and limitations apply. Offer subject to change.

Culture

Northern Lights

Toronto culture is bigger than you think. You see it on movie screens and in high-fashion editorials. You hear it across global airwaves and in underground theaters. You feel it thanks to one of the most empowering punk rock movements in music history.

Screen Double

Long before Toronto became synonymous with glass skyscrapers, filmmakers were using its 20th-century architecture as a stand-in for US cities. The Beaux-Arts and Art Deco towers around Bay Street, the Victorian brick warehouses of the Distillery District, and the Romanesque and Gothic Revival buildings at the *University of Toronto* have all played starring roles.

Even if you've never visited Toronto, you've likely seen it on screen. *Chicago* turned Toronto into the Windy City, with locations like the Distillery District and *Casa Loma* (left). Casa Loma also appears in *X-Men* as the exterior of Xavier's School for Gifted Youngsters, while *Roy Thomson Hall* (above) serves as a futuristic Senate corridor for a confrontation between Professor X and Magneto. The University of Toronto has appeared in several Oscar-winning films, standing in for Harvard in *Good Will Hunting* and for parts of the OCCAM research facility in *The Shape of Water*.

What was the most surprising transformation? That title likely goes to the 2014 *RoboCop* remake, which recast parts of Toronto as a dystopian, near-future Detroit.

• Various locations

Photos: diegograndi

Petra Collins's Star Power

Petra Collins is one of the defining image-makers of contemporary youth culture. Known for her dreamy, pastel-hued visual style, the Toronto-born photographer, director and artist helped define what's been described as the modern "female gaze" in fashion and culture. Collins is also the type of visual storyteller who wants to do more than relive the past with her photo books.

Released in 2026, *Star* follows pop star Ashley and teen-idol group Siren8 through fragmented perspectives, including those of fans and stalkers. The fictional narrative constructs an emotionally charged world where fame and teen stardom distort identity, memory and truth.

Shot largely in her pastel-soaked palette and soft-focus style, *Star* feels dreamlike and deliberately unresolved. At its core, the book continues her exploration of girlhood as both subject and constructed image. The photographs oscillate between staged surrealism and documentary-like immediacy. Bedrooms become stages, bodies become landscapes, and everyday gestures are imbued with quiet theatrics. There is a persistent tension between vulnerability and performance, as her subjects appear both exposed and in control of their own gaze.

Underlying the story is the photographer's own proximity to contemporary pop culture. Collins has shot and directed some of today's biggest pop stars, lending the work a sense of lived-in familiarity with fame. It raises the question of where observation ends and inspiration begins, and how much of the story is drawn from the world she has already documented.

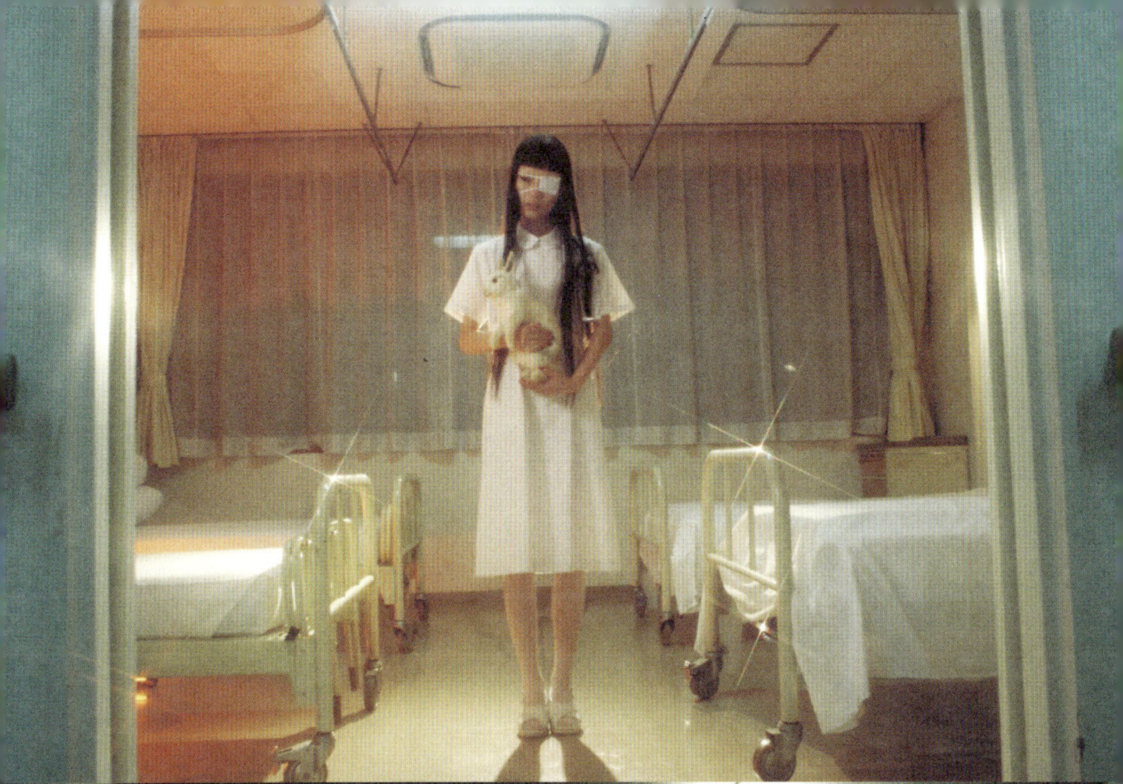

First Nations Rock Star

Toronto-born artist Robbie Robertson (right) was best known as the co-founder and primary songwriter of the Band, one of the most influential groups of the late 1960s and 1970s. He also backed Bob Dylan and created Oscar-nominated music for director Martin Scorsese, from *Raging Bull* (1980) to *Killers of the Flower Moon* (2023). Less widely known is how central his Indigenous heritage was to his identity and storytelling. Mohawk and Cayuga on his mother's side, Robertson spent childhood summers on the Six Nations of the Grand River reserve in Southern Ontario. It was there that the future Rock and Roll Hall of Famer first picked up a guitar and fell in love with storytelling.

Up Close and Personal

Independent performance flourishes in the city's east end, far from the shadow of the Entertainment District's thousand-seat auditoriums. *Coal Mine Theatre*, located in the basement of a former bank, enlists some of Canada's best theater actors to perform hot new scripts. Intimate dramas crackle for audiences of just over a hundred. *The Red Sandcastle Theatre* offers a wilder, more underground experience. It's where Eric Woolfe's house company, *Eldritch Theatre*, performs horror-themed shows filled with puppets and campy theatrical magic. Its bathroom even houses prop shrunken brains.

• Coal Mine Theatre, 2076 Danforth Avenue, coalminetheatre.com; Eldritch Theatre, 922 Queen Street East, eldritchtheatre.ca

Punk Pride

Toronto is widely recognized as a birthplace of queercore, the punk offshoot that emerged in the mid-1980s as a direct rebuke to homophobia, misogyny and the macho culture of the mainstream punk scene. As early as 1981, the all-female band Fifth Column was already pushing against those boundaries, fusing post-punk and noise with explicitly feminist politics. A few years later, Fifth Column member G. B. Jones partnered with Bruce LaBruce to launch the queercore zine *J.D.s* (short for Juvenile Delinquents). Their work helped shape a scene that turned defiance into its own cultural language.

If the zine inspired people to start bands, those bands still needed a place to play. A century-old venue in the Annex became a key stage. In 1985, *Lee's Palace* began hosting live music, providing an early platform for Fifth Column and the emerging queercore scene. Over the years, acts like Oasis, Nirvana and Queens of the Stone Age would also pass through the same stage. But the venue's role in cultivating counterculture didn't end there.

In the early 2000s, Lee's Palace became home to Will Munro's *Vazaleen*, one of the defining queer nightlife institutions in Toronto. Originally launched as Vaseline to the displeasure of the petroleum jelly giant, the party series blurred the line between club night, art project and cultural movement.

Deliberately built as a space for those who didn't fit neatly into either "gay club" norms or straight punk scenes, Vazaleen offered a soundtrack that was chaotic by design. Punk, glam rock, classic metal, indie and pop collided in the same set. The live performances helped amplify a generation of local artists, including Peaches and the Hidden Cameras. Visually, the series was inseparable from its poster culture. Munro, an Ontario College of Art and Design graduate, commissioned artists such as Michael Comeau to produce bold silkscreen flyers that helped define a DIY queer aesthetic that extended well beyond the dance floor.

• Lee's Palace, 529 Bloor Street West, The Annex, leespalace.com

Explore

Toronto

Served All Day

Toronto's food scene is best experienced as a full-day adventure. Start with the markets and specialty shops where local chefs find inspiration, then make your way through the city's diverse neighborhoods before finishing at one of its acclaimed chef-driven restaurants. Along the way, discover the flavors, cultures and ideas that make Toronto one of North America's most exciting culinary destinations.

Mimi Chinese

Start the day as many chefs do at *St. Lawrence Market*, where Toronto cooks and home chefs have sourced ingredients for more than two centuries. Wander through stalls brimming with fresh produce, cheese and specialty food before picking up fresh pastries and your morning coffee from *Luba's Coffee Boutique* or *Everyday Gourmet*.

The Wood Owl

With the market whetting your appetite, it's time for lunch, and no Toronto food tour is complete without exploring its diverse culinary traditions. What piques your interest? You can try royal Thai cuisine at *Kiin*, trendy Caribbean at *Chubby's Jamaican Kitchen* or a modern take on Vietnamese street food at *Banh Mi Boys*. The options are virtually endless, but whatever you choose, you'll earn 2X points at restaurants paying with your Chase Air Canada Aeroplan® Card.

After lunch, spend the afternoon exploring *Kensington Market*, a bohemian neighborhood and longtime incubator for independent restaurants and food businesses. Family-run grocers sit alongside specialty spice shops, bakeries and cafés, reflecting the global influences that have helped shape Toronto's culinary identity.

As evening falls, it's time for the main event: a dinner crafted by one of the city's premier local chefs. Michelin-starred favorites include *Quetzal*, Steven Molnar's fiery Mexican restaurant, and *aKin*, Eric Chong's temple of experimental dining. Toronto is also a top destination for surprising twists on Italian classics. Explore the pan-Asian flavors of *Liliana*, the Jewish-inspired dishes at *N.L. Ginzburg*, or Naples-born Daniele Corona's unique spin on Japanese-Italian itameshi at *DaNico*. For other bold fusion, Craig Wong draws on his Chinese-Jamaican heritage to craft dishes like jerk chicken chow mein at *Patois*. For more classic flavors, *Mimi Chinese* excels at elevated takes on regional Chinese classics in a stylish setting, while *The Wood Owl* shines with seasonal, wine-centric menus in an unpretentious spot in East Toronto. For spots recommended by a chef, Molnar suggests Federico Garcia's *Seahorse* and one of his former culinary homes, the Spanish-inspired *Bar Raval*.

If you still have energy for a nightcap, finish the evening with an award-winning cocktail at the renowned *Bar Pompette* or slip into one of the city's stylish speakeasies like *à toi*, hidden behind a secret door at *Coffee Oysters Champagne*.

Quetzal

The only guarantee on a culinary tour of Toronto? There will always be more to taste on your next visit. Whether you're already planning new reservations in Toronto or setting your sights on another culinary destination, cardmembers earn up to 5X total points on Air Canada purchases and receive up to $100 in Air Canada statement credits annually. For smoother travel experiences, you'll also enjoy Priority Check-In, free first checked bags and Priority Boarding (Zone 2) with automatic Elite Status. This card is available exclusively to qualified individuals with a U.S. address.

Where should you go next? With Air Canada's 180+ destinations and over 1,300 destinations across its 45+ global airline partners, the world is your menu.

Scan or learn more at chase.com/aircanadacard

Worlds of Escape

From underground bathhouses to Turkish steam rituals, the local spa scene offers three distinct paths to the same goal: total escape.

Photo: AIRE

Deep Soak

Deep underground, behind the labyrinth of Portland Commons, lies an unexpected nirvana. *AIRE Ancient Baths Toronto* follows the company's tradition of transforming restored warehouse spaces into heavenly wellness experiences. Exposed brick walls and backlit factory windows tell the story of the venue's previous life as a publishing company, perfectly renovated into an industrial oasis. The entire venue is a cell phone–free space, allowing you to truly relax. Space is limited, so reserve a time in advance.

• Aire Ancient Baths, 510A Front Street West, Wellington Place, relax.beaire.com

Lap of Luxury

Finding a high-end spa inside a five-star hotel is no surprise, but the *Spa at the Four Seasons* somehow continues to amaze. The serene and sparkling facility offers everything needed by a traveler looking to luxuriate. There's a steam room and fitness suite; private spaces for massages, facials and scrubs; and, of course, the pool. Spa amenities are available to all patrons, though family pool hours are limited to guests of the hotel for maximum comfort. Every detail has been carefully considered, creating the perfect environment to truly unwind.

• Spa at the Four Seasons, 60 Yorkville Avenue, The Annex, fourseasons.com/toronto/spa

Steam Clean

In the heart of Queen West sits a quiet sanctuary to steam your troubles away. *Hammam Spa by Céla* is a Toronto brand inspired by ancient Turkish hammam rituals. The star of both locations is the large, tiled steam room, with rejuvenating eucalyptus oils and included light therapies. The spa offers full packages with facials, scrubs and, of course, massages, but if you're simply looking for a relaxing steam and cup of tea to break up your day, shorter visits are an option.

• Hammam Spa by Céla, 602 King Street West, Wellington Place, hammamspa.ca

Photo: The Four Seasons Toronto

Editors' Picks

Street Cred

From hand-held dishes to designer threads, these picks reveal how Toronto's creative community takes street culture to the next level.

6ix Streetwear

Toronto's streetwear scene is shaped by utilitarian design and deep hip-hop roots. October's Very Own, or OVO, was co-founded by Drake for music releases and artist merchandise before pivoting to a stand-alone fashion brand. It set the tone early, turning its owl-branded loungewear (photo) into a global shorthand for Toronto identity and pride. Today, a new wave of designers pushes past basic merch into high-fashion storytelling. Adidem Asterisks* bridges sport, community and collegiate prep, delivering everyday styles that capture the city's cultural rhythm. Meanwhile, Spencer Badu pushes a stripped-back, postgender approach defined by clean lines, modular construction and precise tailoring. Together, these labels signal a shift from merch to meaning in Toronto streetwear.

- octobersveryown.com, adidem.world, spencerbadu.com

X Marks the Hot

XOXO Sauce is a rich, umami-packed condiment created by Liliana chef Marvin Palomo. Inspired by traditional XO sauce from his time cooking in Hong Kong and later refined in Toronto, this cult favorite is built on a base of dried shrimp, scallop, chili, peanut oil and aromatics. What started as a pandemic passion project has evolved into a pantry staple, delivering a balanced sweet-spicy-savory punch to everything from noodles and rice dishes to grilled meats and vegetables.

- XOXO, xoxosauce.ca

Read

Cat's Eye
• Margaret Atwood, 1988

Cat's Eye follows a celebrated but controversial painter who returns to Toronto for a retrospective of her work, a homecoming that triggers haunting memories of her childhood and the bullying she endured from her peers in the mid-20th century.

In the Skin of a Lion
• Michael Ondaatje, 1987

Blending near-mythic storytelling with deep archival research, Michael Ondaatje (*The English Patient*) illuminates the lives of immigrant laborers who built the city's defining infrastructure. Through vivid portraits of bridge workers, tunnel diggers and social outsiders, the novel uncovers the human stories often missing from the history books.

The Torontonians
• Phyllis Brett Young, 1960

One of the biggest hits of its era, *The Torontonians* captured suburban discontent with uncanny precision. The book follows a housewife living in an affluent suburb surrounded by manicured lawns, cocktail parties and the promise of postwar prosperity. Despite living "the dream," she finds herself increasingly trapped by the quiet anxieties that simmer beneath her picture-perfect life.

Watch

Videodrome
• David Cronenberg, 1983

Set against the grimy backdrop of pre-gentrification Toronto, *Videodrome* is a cult classic that blurs the boundaries between television, technology and reality. The story follows a cynical cable TV programmer who uncovers a rogue broadcast signal that triggers hallucinations and bodily transformations.

Goin' Down the Road
• Donald Shebib, 1970

Goin' Down the Road follows young men who leave rural Nova Scotia in pursuit of a better life in Toronto. Instead of the prosperity they imagined, they are met with the harsh realities of low-wage labor, housing insecurity and mounting disillusionment. The film serves as a gritty portrait of Toronto at a pivotal moment of rapid growth and social change.

Exotica
• Atom Egoyan, 1994

Within the walls of a strip club, a group of broken lives intersect as the film slowly unspools a web of grief, obsession and haunting memory. Through fragmented storytelling and rhythmic repetition, *Exotica* explores the depths of trauma, voyeurism and the paper-thin boundaries between intimacy and exploitation.

Spin

"City of Mirrors"
• BADBADNOTGOOD, 2021

"City of Mirrors" blends jazz textures with chill hip-hop rhythms, with a music video that follows street skaters carving lines through the city. The trio has built a reputation for genre-blurring collaboration, earning their first Grammy for Kendrick Lamar's "LUST." Tracks with Ghostface Killah, MF DOOM and Tyler, the Creator further infuse jazz with a modern edge rooted in sonic experimentation.

"The Anthem"
• Kardinal Offishall, 2010

Long before Drake's groundbreaking mixtape, Kardinal Offishall blew the doors open for Canadian rap with a sound rooted in his Caribbean heritage. At peak fame, the Toronto native dropped "The Anthem" as a fierce rallying cry for the city's culture and swagger. A defining tribute to the city, the standalone single captures Toronto as an identity: loud, confident and unifying.

"Born in Ontario"
• Neil Young, 2012

Neil Young, a rock legend with several Grammy wins and Hall of Fame inductions, paid tribute to his roots with the reflective "Born in Ontario." Backed by the folk-rock grooves of his longtime band, Crazy Horse, Young weaves personal memories into the broader Canadian landscape, tracing formative spaces and experiences.